Goodheart-Willcox's BUILD-A-COURSE® Series

graphic arts

by

FREDERICK D. KAGY

Department of Industrial Technology
Illinois State University, Normal

WALTER C. BROWN, Consulting Editor

Professor, Division of Technology
Arizona State University, Tempe

Books in Build-A-Course® Series

Woodworking — Wagner

Drafting — Brown

Electricity — Gerrish

Metalworking — Boyd

Modern General Shop

Graphic Arts — Kagy

Power Mechanics — Atteberry

Leathercraft — Zimmerman

Plastics — Cope and Schaude

South Holland, Illinois
THE GOODHEART-WILLCOX COMPANY, INC.
Publishers

INTRODUCTION

Graphic arts is a broad field of work which includes many activities in an ever-advancing technology. The purpose of this course is to help you explore graphic arts. As a part of your general education, it will acquaint you with composition fundamentals, basic mechanics of all types of printing and the essential elements found in all printed pieces.

Automation, computers, new machines and new methods are changing the traditional field of printing. While much of the labor in graphic arts has changed from an art to a manufacturing science, the skill and knowledge of the printer is still important in turning out quality products. It is more necessary than ever that those wishing to work in the graphic arts understand the basic processes. Only with a thorough grounding in the fundamentals will they understand and adapt to technological change.

This revised edition is entirely reorganized and accurately represents the revolution that has occurred in printing processes. A completely new and reorganized content introduces current theory and practice of the graphic communications industry.

Graphic communications is a vital link in the exchange of ideas between the many parts of business and industry. It offers satisfying careers and steady employment to qualified workers who are well paid. When deciding on your future work, this important field warrants careful consideration.

Frederick D. Kagy

Copyright 1987

by

THE GOODHEART-WILLCOX COMPANY, INC.

Previous Editions Copyright 1981, 1978, 1970, 1965, 1961

Library of Congress Catalog Card Number 87-238
International Standard Book Number 0-87006-646-3

123456789-87-543210987

Library of Congress Cataloging in Publication Data

Kagy, Frederick D.
  Graphic arts.

  (Goodheart-Willcox's build-a-course series)
  Includes index.
  1. Graphic arts.   2. Printing, Practical.
I. Title.   II. Series.
Z244.K25   1987   686.2'2   87-238
ISBN 0-87006-646-3

CONTENTS

CAREERS IN GRAPHIC ARTS

UNIT 1

1. The size and nature of the graphic arts industry.
2. Job opportunities in graphic arts and related fields.
3. Entering the graphic arts field.

The graphic arts play an important part in our lives. We communicate using the graphic arts. To be sure, there are others ways to find out what is taking place around us. We have television and radio and we can talk to our friends.

It is often difficult to remember all that is said or seen, either live or on radio and television. By having messages and ideas printed, we can save them to read again and again. Or we can read them over several times before we discard the printed matter.

More than 40,000 companies are engaged in some kind of graphic arts service. Some produce only a single product or service. Others are large companies which provide many products or services. Some may provide only one product, such as books, but carry on all the processes within the company.

You are probably very much aware of some companies in the graphic arts industry. They are the ones that produce the comic books, newspapers, books, photographs and posters that you see every day. You also know such products as business forms, greeting cards, bank checks, billboard signs, and printed packaging materials such as boxes, cans and wrapping paper.

Other printing businesses are not as well known. One group is those companies that specialize in one or several processes for publishers. Examples are:

1. Engravers who produce halftones and press plates ready for printing.
2. Companies that set type only.
3. Companies that fold, gather and bind printing material such as brochures, magazines and books.
4. Firms that produce photographs and photostats.
5. Firms that create art and design printed pieces.

Related to printing are firms which make printing equipment and materials. They supply presses, paper, inks, films and papers. See Fig. 1-1.

WHERE THE GRAPHIC ARTS INDUSTRY IS FOUND

Graphic arts industry is found just about everywhere. Certain cities are known as graphic arts centers. There are few counties in any state that do not have a newspaper or some kind of commercial printing plant. Many companies maintain a graphic arts department to print their own forms, envelopes, newspapers and flyers, even though their products have nothing to do with printing.

Possibly there are graphic arts companies in your community. They will vary in size and appearance. Some may be housed in huge buildings. Some may be small, one or two-person operations. Most cities will have newspapers.

One of the fastest growing areas in printing is the in-plant shop. Both large and small businesses have them. They produce the forms, catalogs, sales materials and stationery used by the company.

Fig. 1-1. This mammoth machine makes paper in continuous rolls. About 700,000 people are employed to produce paper and paper products in the U.S.

JOB OPPORTUNITIES

The graphic arts industry employs more than 400,000 people with a variety of interests and talents. These talents and skills are grouped around several clusters of jobs.

CREATIVE TASKS

Persons holding creative jobs work up ideas to some form of visual or written message. In this group are artists, writers, reporters, authors, editors, designers, illustrators and photographers.

Creative people are able to express ideas visually. Editors, writers, reporters and authors do it with words. Writers will read up on the subject, gather illustrations and prepare copy or manuscripts. Editors help writers develop their ideas. They polish the final written material and prepare instructions on how it should be typeset. See Fig. 1-2. They will also mark instructions on the illustrations and decide on their size.

Designers, Fig. 1-3, produce illustrations and arrange attractive printed pieces. They design covers for books and retouch photographs. They produce charts and maps.

Photographers produce pictures using a camera. Their work combines art knowledge with knowledge of cameras, film, chemicals and paper. Like the designer, they will arrange elements in the picture before they expose the film.

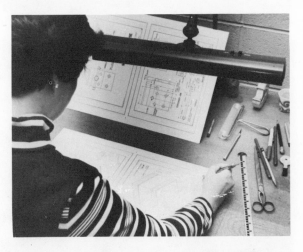

Fig. 1-3 Designer preparing drawings for the printer.

MANAGEMENT TASKS

Executives and supervisors organize machines, materials and skills to make them work well together. They are the leaders and directors in a company. See Fig. 1-4. Those working as managers direct the work of others. They think about ways of doing things and pick the best method.

TECHNICAL TASKS

Some work areas require high-level skills. Those who do such work must know a great deal about properties of materials and have considerable ability

Fig. 1-4. Manager of a print shop schedules printing jobs as part of his work.

in mathematics. We call them technicians. They work in such areas as quality control, computer programming, cost estimating and research. Two examples of the technician's work are:

1. Testing of inks and paper. Using instruments, the technician will find out how these materials will react to printing condition. This will help in

Fig. 1-2. An editor at work revising a textbook.

selecting the right material for the printing job.

2. Producing instructions so a computer will set type. This is called programming. The technician must use special coding and follow certain steps so the computer will perform the work.

Other work done by the technician includes:

1. Preparing formal reports.
2. Assisting scientists and engineers in developing new equipment or new products.
3. Setting up, calibrating and operating instruments.
4. Preparing sales brochures.

PRODUCTION TASKS

Many skilled persons are needed at various stages of printing. In larger graphic arts operations, workers will specialize. The work can be divided into clearly defined areas. The first is called IMAGE GENERATION. It includes design and layout, composition, photography and plate preparation.

Another area of specialization is called IMAGE TRANSFER. In this stage, the plate is put on the press, the press is adjusted and the printing is done. Finally, the printed job is folded, bound and trimmed. This area is called FINISHING.

Those who set type are called COMPOSITORS or TYPESETTERS. Working from typed copy, they set type by hand or operate a keyboard for lead casting or phototypesetting equipment. Some compositors are called CRT (cathode ray tube) OPERATORS, Fig. 1-5. These machines set type from information stored in computers. When the compositor operates a machine which casts type in lead, he or she is called a LINOTYPE OPERATOR. Sometimes, the setting of cold type is referred to as "keyboarding."

Fig. 1-5. This compositor is using a phototypesetter to set text material. (Compugraphic)

Letterpress printers may employ electrotypers and STEREOTYPERS. They make duplicate press plates from metal, rubber and plastic.

Graphic arts today is heavily tied to photography. CAMERA OPERATORS photograph copy and process the film used to transfer the image to printing plates. ARTISTS retouch film negatives to correct imperfections. They use chemicals, dyes and hand tools.

Fig. 1-6. Stripper prepares film negative, attaching it to special paper for burning (exposing) press plate.

STRIPPERS, Fig. 1-6, prepare film for exposing the press plate. They attach the film to light-proof sheets called "goldenrod." PLATEMAKERS transfer the film image to sensitized metal plates which will be attached to the press cylinder.

PRINTERS or PRESS OPERATORS attach plates to the press cylinder and run the job. Adjustments are made for image position and ink flow, Fig. 1-7.

Bookbinders or bindery workers are highly skilled machine operators who set and operate folding, gathering, sewing, stitching and casing machinery. Printed materials can be made into brochures, pamphlets, magazines and books that are glued, sewed or spiral bound in metal or plastic. Fig. 1-8 shows a bindery operation.

Fig. 1-7. One operator is needed for a simple offset press.

GRAPHIC ARTS SALES

Selling the equipment, supplies, services and products of graphic arts is a valuable activity for persons who like to meet and persuade other people. The salesperson brings together those who make and those who need these commodities.

A person working in this field might be selling art or design skills, typesetting, printing, film, ink or advertising space in a magazine or newspaper.

TEACHING GRAPHIC ARTS

Training others for graphic arts skills is a very satisfying profession for some who like to work with people. Such jobs are offered by high school industrial arts programs, vocational schools or by colleges and universities which train teachers, Fig. 1-9. Previous job experience in the graphic arts is helpful but not required.

Fig. 1-8. View of bindery operation which gathers, attaches covers and trims book in one assembly line. (Semline, Inc.)

Fig. 1-9. Teaching graphic arts skills is a satisfying profession.

ENTERING THE FIELD

Some graphic arts jobs require several months or years of training at vocational schools, community colleges or universities. The most common method of entering the field is through on-the-job training. Often, this is combined with a formal apprenticeship program.

Usually, apprentices must have a high school education or its equivalent. Ability to spell and punctuate are valuable assets. So is an understanding of grammar. Being able to use a typewriter is helpful, too. Your instructor or a counselor will assist you in selecting courses most useful in a graphic arts career.

The wages paid by the graphic arts industry are good. The industry is typically not seriously affected by recessions and layoffs. The graphic arts industry has a great and lasting effect on the economics, education and heritage of our country.

QUIZ — UNIT 1

1. More than 4000 companies are involved in the printing industry. True or False?
2. Name three kinds of companies that supply services to publishers.
3. A _____ is one who can organize workers and machines so they will work efficiently.
4. Which of the printing occupations described in this unit would you like to try?
5. List ways of entering the graphic arts industry.

FUNDAMENTALS OF PRINTING PROCESSES

1. Introducing the four conventional printing processes: lithography, letterpress, intaglio and screen process.
2. And seven special printing processes: electrostatic printing, copying, office duplicating, stencil duplication, three-dimensional printing, sublimation printing and ink jet printing.
3. Identifying the three areas of work in production printing.

Printing is basically a means of using INK to transfer IMAGES arranged on a PRESS PLATE to paper, metal, glass, plastic or some other material. Some special types of printing use powders, heat or chemicals to place an image on the material. Another method of image production, not always thought of as printing, is photography.

CONVENTIONAL PRINTING METHODS

Printing methods can be grouped according to the principles on which their image carriers or printing plates are based. Most large-volume printing jobs will use one of the following printing methods:

1. LITHOGRAPHY, also called planographic or offset printing.
2. RELIEF PRINTING, also called letterpress.
3. INTAGLIO or gravure printing.
4. SCREEN PROCESS or silk screen printing.

LITHOGRAPHIC (OFFSET) PRINTING

In lithography, the image carrier or press plate is a smooth metal sheet. Its surface is flat. The area which carries the printing ink is at the same level as the area which does not have ink on it. See Fig. 2-1.

LITHOGRAPHIC PRINCIPLES

The lithographic process works even though the press plate has no raised images. It uses moisture and greasy materials (inks) to separate the image area from the non-image area. The FOUNTAIN SOLUTION (mostly water) clings to the non-image area but

Fig. 2-1. In lithographic printing, the paper is pressed against a flat, inked plate. Only greasy image areas will hold ink.

is repelled by the greasy image area. Ink clings to the image area and transfers to the first surface it touches as the press cylinder turns. The ink and fountain solutions are applied automatically by the printing press as the press plate revolves on the plate cylinder. The plate is dampened with water and inked each time the cylinder makes a complete turn.

OFFSET METHOD

While it is possible to print directly from the lithographic plate, the most popular method is to transfer the inked image from the plate to a second cylinder. It is called the BLANKET or offset cylinder. The blanket is like a hard sponge and it accepts the ink from the press plate. Then, as the sheet of printing paper (or other material which is to receive the image) passes between the blanket and the IMPRESSION roller, the ink is transferred or offset to the sheet.

Because the ink moves from press plate to blanket to paper the process is called OFFSET LITHO-GRAPHIC printing. A diagram of the press arrangement is shown in Fig. 2-2.

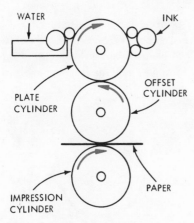

Fig. 2-2. Part of the offset press showing the arrangement of cylinders in a three-cylinder press. The sheet of paper passes between the smooth impression roller and the blanket or offset roller.

Offset presses print on sheets or a continuous roll called a web of paper. Some presses operate with two cylinders; others use three cylinders.

The offset printing plate can be made from many different materials. Among them are metal, aluminum and zinc, paper and plastic.

RELIEF OR LETTERPRESS PRINTING

In RELIEF or LETTERPRESS PRINTING, the image (words and pictures) is raised above the nonprinting areas. Fig. 2-3 shows this. The ink is applied only to the raised areas by the inking rollers. The raised surface may be type which has been set by hand or machine, engraving made from copper, zinc, magnesium, wood, rubber, plastic or a combination of these materials.

No single diagram could show the various designs of printing presses used in relief printing. The major types are:

1. The PLATEN PRESS. Paper is fed to a flat surface called a platen. The platen contacts the inked type

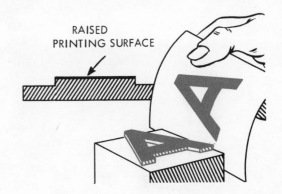

Fig. 2-3. Image areas are raised in the letter press plate.

form clamped against the bed of the press, Fig. 2-4. It uses a "clapping" motion to press the sheet of paper against the surface carrying the image. Although the platen press is an old design, it is still used often in small job printing shops as well as in school shops.

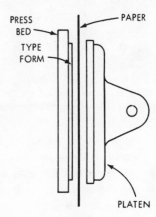

Fig. 2-4. With paper sandwiched between them, the type form and the platen squeeze together so that the ink transfers from the type to the paper.

2. The FLAT BED CYLINDER PRESS. Paper is held on a cylinder by means of metal "fingers" called grippers. The cylinder rolls over the printed form locked on a flat bed as in Fig. 2-5. The printing form moves horizontally and the paper revolves with the cylinder over the form.
3. The ROTARY PRESS. Both paper and plates are on cylinders rolling against each other, Fig. 2-6. The plates — sterotypes or electrotypes — are curved to fit the cylinders. Paper used for printing on a rotary press may be in sheets (sheet fed press) or in rolls (web fed press).

INTAGLIO PRINTING

INTAGLIO or gravure printing uses a depressed or sunken surface for transferring ink to the paper. See

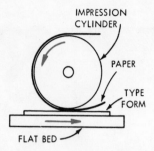

Fig. 2-5. Principle of flat bed press. As sheet is printed, the bed holding the type forms, moves in the same direction as the surface of the cylinder.

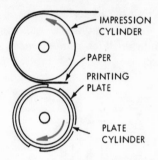

Fig. 2-6. Principle of rotary press. Cylinders press against each other as paper is carried between them.

Fig. 2-7. A copper plate, curved to fit the press cylinder, is etched with depressions of different depth. These pits act as wells to hold small deposits of ink that are transferred to the paper during printing.

During the inking process, ink is applied to the entire plate. Then the surface is wiped or scraped by a

metal blade so that ink remains only in the depressions or image areas.

During printing, suction lifts the ink out of the depressions onto the paper. Like rotary letterpress, gravure presses are made for both sheets and rolls. The paper is pressed against the inked plate, Fig. 2-8.

SCREEN PROCESS PRINTING

Screen printing is vastly different from the other conventional processes of printing. In this method, Fig. 2-9, the printing liquid (ink, paint or other fluid) is forced through a fine mesh screen made of cloth or metal.

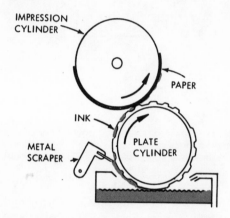

Fig. 2-8. In gravure or intaglio printing, image area of plate holds ink in tiny "wells" until transferred to paper.

The design is first created on a stencil. This is usually a gelatinous material coated on a backing fabric of mylar or waxed paper. The design is made in the stencil and then the stencil is attached to the screen. Simple stencils for school use can be made from kraft paper.

Fig. 2-7. Printing surface in intaglio printing is below rest of printing plate.

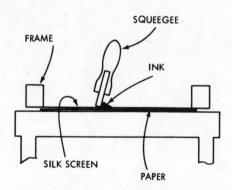

Fig. 2-9. Silk screen process. Rubber blade of the squeegee forces ink through mesh of screen onto print surface.

A squeegee forces the fluid through the screen in the image areas of the stencil where the stencil material has been removed. The design is produced by removing the stencil material either by hand or photographically.

Silk screen printing works well on paper, metal, wood or various other surfaces. In its simplest form, it is a hand process. Use of special, faster equipment makes it a useful commercial process where large volume is needed. It is also known as "porous printing."

SPECIAL PRINTING PROCESSES

The need of modern industry for rapid, inexpensive and small-volume reproduction of visual materials has given rise to a number of special processes. These are called special printing processes. They differ from conventional printing in several ways:

1. The vehicle, or material which is transferred, may not be ink. It may be a dry powder magnetized to stick to the paper, chemicals which react with other chemicals or heat, or a variation of these two vehicles.
2. The process may be more or less automatic allowing unskilled workers to use it successfully.
3. The quality of reproduction is generally not as good as conventional printing.

ELECTROSTATIC PRINTING

Like screen printing, ELECTROSTATIC PRINTING applies the principle of porous printing, Fig. 2-10. It is also referred to as pressureless printing

because the image-forming element or plate need not touch the image receiving surface. Thus, materials with uneven surfaces can be printed by this method.

In electrostatic printing, a thin plate is prepared with the design. The plate allows finely powdered, magnetically charged pigment particles to be metered through the image opening.

The particles attach themselves to the surface being printed. Electrostatic attraction holds the particles to the print surface until heat or chemicals fuse them permanently to the material.

COPYING

There are many processes designed to make single duplicate copies or copies in limited numbers. These, too, must be included as a part of graphic communications, while not considered printing by conventional standards.

All copying processes fall into four general groups:

1. Wet process copiers.
2. Heat process copiers.
3. Diazo process copiers, Fig. 2-11.
4. Electrostatic process copiers, Fig. 2-12.

Many manufacturers produce copy machines. They have become an important addition to businesses where one or a few copies are needed instantly.

OFFICE DUPLICATING

Office duplicators are sometimes table top versions of larger presses. While not considered to be con-

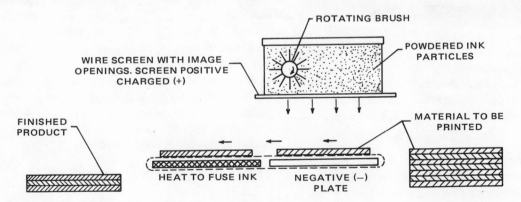

Fig. 2-10. Electrostatic printing works on principle that unlike electrical charges attract while like charges repel. Powder is positively charged while plate has a negative charge.

Fig. 2-11. White printer is popular for reproducing architectural and machine drawings used in industry. It uses the diazo process.   (Teledyne Post)

Fig. 2-12. Electrostatic copier uses electrically charged powdered ink and heat to produce a printed image.   (Xerox Corp.)

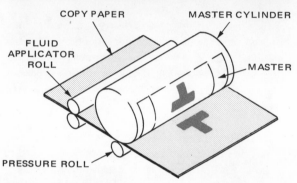

Fig. 2-13. Spirit duplicating. Top. Desk top duplicators are used in schools and offices. Bottom. Dampened with solvent, paper softens and picks up carbon from master placed on cylinder.   (A.B. Dick)

ventional printing, office duplication has a definite place in producing graphic communication. The processes are important for certain types of small-run interoffice work.

The SPIRIT DUPLICATOR process, Fig. 2-13, uses a reverse master (image carrier). Liquid on the sheet of paper being printed dissolves and picks up carbon from the image area of the master. When the carbon is gone, the master is discarded.

The MIMEOGRAPH duplicating process, often called stencil duplicating, is an efficient and inexpensive method of graphic communication. The image carrier is a sheet of porous tissue that has been coated on both sides with a wax material. The wax material does not permit passage of the ink.

The image is placed on the stencil by typewriter and a special stylus. Typing on the stencil displaces the wax coating so that ink can pass through the porous tissue base.

A completed stencil is wrapped around the drum of the mimeograph duplicator, Fig. 2-14. The drum is porous underneath the stencil. Ink is placed inside the drum and passes through the drum and stencil onto the printing paper as the drum rotates.

THREE-DIMENSIONAL PRINTING

Printing is two-dimensional, having width and height. A special process has been developed which

SUBLIMATION PRINTING

The process used to print designs on cloth is called SUBLIMATION or heat transfer printing. While most people think of it as the type of printing shown in Fig. 2-15, this process is also used to put decorative designs on fabrics.

Fig. 2-15. Sublimation printing. Transfer sheet at left is printed by any of the major printing processes. Under heat and pressure, the special ink turns to a gas and the color transfers to the cloth as at right.

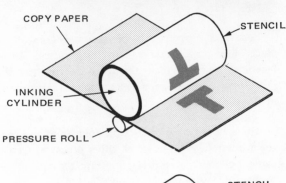

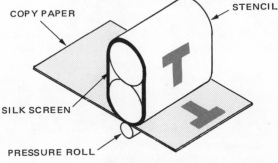

Fig. 2-14. Top. Mimeograph machines are inexpensive and can be operated electrically or by hand. Bottom. Principle parts are inking cylinder and pressure roller. Pad between stencil and drum releases ink through stencil upon pressure from pressure roller. (A.B. Dick)

The nature of the ink used is the secret of its success. The ink is printed in reverse on a piece of transfer paper. Any of the major printing methods can be used for this part of the process.

In the next step of the process, the cloth to be printed is placed in a heat press with the printed design in the proper position. Heat and pressure transfers the design. The special ink changes into a gaseous state and "goes into" the fibers of the cloth. When cooled, the design becomes nearly permanent.

INK JET PRINTING

INK JET PRINTING prints images on paper using an entirely new technology. This process prints directly from information stored in a computer.

The printing unit consists of a series of ink jets which are made to drop ink in a controlled pattern. A single jet is shown in Fig. 2-16.

The information stored in the computer, operates the ink jet units. Some of the ink drops become electrically charged while others do not. The charged

gives a third dimension of depth. A printed image is broken up into stereoscopic components. (In simpler language, it divides the image into what might be seen separately by each eye.) A sheet of plastic is placed on top of this image to divide the picture into hundreds of tiny vertical strips.

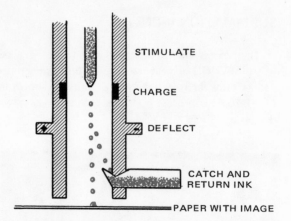

STIMULATE

CHARGE

DEFLECT

CATCH AND
RETURN INK

PAPER WITH IMAGE

Fig. 2-16. Ink jet printing. Jet lets down droplets on command from computer. Charged particles are collected and return to the ink supply. Noncharged droplets apply the image to the paper.

drops are deflected and return to the ink supply. The uncharged drops go down to the paper to produce an image. Several manufacturers are producing these machines and each system is slightly different.

Ink jet systems are being used to print direct mail advertising. They are also found to be an efficient way of addressing mailing pieces in large volume, Fig. 2-17.

Fig. 2-17. Videojet printer provides high-speed addressing of newspapers and magazines.
(A.B. Dick Information Products Div.)

DIVIDING GRAPHIC ARTS WORK

Basically, there are three distinct areas of work in the production of printed pieces:

1. PREPRESS WORK. This area includes art and copy preparation and conversion into printing image carriers.
2. PRESSWORK which includes methods of image transfer.
3. POSTPRESS WORK. This operation includes binding and finishing.

These areas of work are usually carried on in three different departments. The prepress area is often called the composing room. It is here, that type is set and photos or illustrations assembled into a form that can either be reproduced on a press, or photographed by a camera.

Presswork is done in the pressroom where workers place the image carriers in the presses. These machines are run to make the image transfer from the inked image carrier to the paper. Paper can be printed in sheets or rolls.

The bindery department will fold, bind and trim the printed sheets of material. Other processes such as gathering, collating, drilling, inserting, die cutting and packaging may be done in the bindery.

Later units will explain many of these processes.

QUIZ – UNIT 2

1. Printing is a means of using _____ to transfer _____ on a press _____ to some type of material.
2. Name four printing methods.
3. In lithography, the printing image is raised above the surface of the printing plate. True or False?
4. In letterpress, of what materials are the engravings made?
5. Intaglio printing uses _____ surface for transferring ink to paper.
6. Draw a sketch showing how silk screening is done.
7. In _____ printing finely powdered, electrically charged particles of ink are metered through the image openings.
8. A new process which uses heat to transfer ink to cloth is called _____ printing.

DESIGN AND LAYOUT

UNIT 3

1. Using design to produce a printed message.
2. Identifying different styles of type.
3. Preparing a printing layout.

Printing has one purpose. It carries a message. The message tells us a story, instructs us or asks us to do something. It must be attractive and easy to read. If it is not, the message will not be received. The job of design is to make sure the printing looks good. It should make people want to read it.

Design is not usually the printer's job. Most printing is designed by the person who is buying printing (client). The layout may have been prepared by:

1. An agency.
2. An artist working for the buyer.
3. A layout department in the printing company.

Still, we must talk about the need for good planning. To plan well for printing, we should know about design, type selection and layout.

THE ART OF DESIGNING

Design is the process of deciding how a piece of printing will look. The design is done before any type is set. It is done before illustrations are made or picked.

Designing follows certain steps and uses certain rules. It answers questions a printer needs to ask about size, shape, style, color and cost.

Before the designer plans a piece of printing, the following must be known:

1. What is the purpose of the message?
2. For whom is it intended?
3. How will the message reach the receiver?

4. What money, equipment and materials are available to produce this message?

DESIGN ELEMENTS

Design elements are all the things you see on the printed page. They are the ways in which the designer shapes the message on paper. Elements consist of:

1. Line. Lines are seen as thick, thin, horizontal, curved, wavy, slanted or looped. They can help organize the message. They can move the eye up, down, to the left or to the right. See Fig. 3-1.
2. Form or shapes. To create form, the designer combines some of the lines just mentioned. Form gives body to the ideas presented. The forms can be rectangles, squares, pyramids, triangles, circles or irregular shapes, Fig. 3-2.
3. Mass. How big elements look. Amount of space taken up. Darker shapes look heavier, Fig. 3-3.
4. Color. Color adds meaning to the message by making some parts of it stand out. See Fig. 3-4.
5. Texture. It has to do with the roughness or smoothness of a material. For example, the paper used to carry the message can be glossy, dull, soft or bumpy.

DESIGN PRINCIPLES

The principles of design are followed so that printed messages have a pleasant look. The principles give the designer direction and guidance, but do not tie her or him down to a set of rules that must be followed. The principles are:

1. Proportion. This is the fitness of the relationship between the various parts and the whole design.

A well planned graphic arts shop in a school will include offset press equipment. A photo-offset printing unit consists of an ink fountain and rollers, a water fountain and rollers, and three large metal cylinders. The printing plate is attached to the top cylinder; a rubber blanket is attached to the center cylinder, and the bottom cylinder carries the paper through the press, forcing it against the rubber blanket to make a printed impression. When the press is turned on, the cylinders revolve, and the plate is carried under the dampen-

A good graphic arts shop in a school will include offset press equipment. A photo-offset printing unit consists of an ink fountain and rollers, a water fountain and rollers, and three large metal cylinders. The printing plate is attached to the top cylinder; a rubber blanket is

A well planned graphic arts shop in a school will include offset press equipment. A photo-offset printing unit consists of an ink fountain and rollers, a water fountain and rollers, and three large metal cylinders. The printing plate is attached to the top cylinder; a rubber blanket is attached to the center cylinder, and the bottom cylinder carries the paper through the press, forcing it against the rubber blanket to make a printed impression. When the press is turned on, the cylinders revolve, and the plate is carried under the dampening rollers, the inking rollers, and finally against the rubber blanket. The

Fig. 3-1. Lines may be any size, length, weight or shape.

Fig. 3-2. Lines can be combined to form shapes. Blocks of copy also give form or shape.

Parts must seem to belong together. The size of each part must seem right. See Fig. 3-5.

2. Balance. Every element in a printing layout has weight. When the weight of one element is offset by the weight of another, you have elements in balance. Imagine two children on a seesaw. If they are the same size, they can sit the same distance from the center. If one is heavier, he or she must sit nearer the center than the other. In both cases you have balance. Balance can be formal (symmetrical) as in Fig. 3-6 or informal as in Fig. 3-7.

3. Emphasis. A page of type looks very boring if all the type is the same size and there are no other elements that stand out. Emphasis makes a certain

Fig. 3-3. How principle of mass is used in design. Left. Geometric shapes with colored mass as center of interest. Lower right. Blackness draws attention in company names. (Heidelberg Eastern, Inc. and Midland-Ross Corp.)

 FIVE MAIN CAMERA ELEMENTS

1. Camera body. A light-proof box with a device to hold the film at one end. An opening at the opposite end is designed to hold a lens.

2. Lens. Essentially, this is a piece of glass shaped so that it changes the direction of the rays of light coming through it. As the rays fall on the light-sensitive film at the camera back, they form an image from light reflected by the camera subject.

3. Shutter. A movable cover that is usually closed to keep out light. But it opens for a fraction of a second to allow light to enter through the lens and fall on the film.

4. Shutter release. A lever or plunger which trips a shutter.

5. A "peep sight" to show you what you will get on your picture.

Fig. 3-4. Color is used to add emphasis to the printed message.

OUT OF PROPORTION
WORM TOO SMALL

IN PROPORTION
APPLE AND WORM RIGHT
FOR EACH OTHER

OUT OF PROPORTION
WORM TOO BIG

Fig. 3-5. Sizes of different parts must be right for good proportion.

part of the total design more important. It can be achieved by use of color, size, style of type or size of illustration. See Fig. 3-8.

4. Unity or harmony ties together the layout elements. Without it, the design falls apart and the message is lost, Fig. 3-9.

5. Rhythm gives direction by repeating a certain form, Fig. 3-10.

Not all designs use every principle. Nor are principles always easy to identify. In some printed pieces, two or more design principles may overlap. Principles should not be allowed to give a new designer problems. They are starting places for the beginner. If the design is pleasing, follow it through.

Fig. 3-6. Formal balance is present when both sides of an imaginary vertical center line are equally weighted with elements of the message.

Fig. 3-7. Informal balance has elements on one side heavier than the other side. Here the type element is lighter but contrast provided by the reverse adds weight to the type area.

Fig. 3-8. Emphasis provides a point of interest in a design. Eye is drawn to it because it stands out over other elements.

TYPE IDENTIFICATION

After the general plan or design is made, the next step is to select the type that will be used to present the message. For the designer, as well as the printer, it is important to be familiar with typefaces. Names of the parts of a typeface are shown in Fig. 3-11.

Lines which form the letters are known as strokes. The lighter lines are called light elements. The heavier lines are called heavy elements. Crosslines at the ends of the elements are called serifs.

There is more than one way of identifying type styles. But the system most often used is to group them into six basic styles:

1. Roman.
   a. Old style.
   b. Modern.
   c. Transitional.
2. Text.
3. Square serif.
4. Sans serif (no serifs).
5. Script.
6. Decorative.

Fig. 3-12 shows samples of all six styles. If you were to look at type catalogs you would find many more examples.

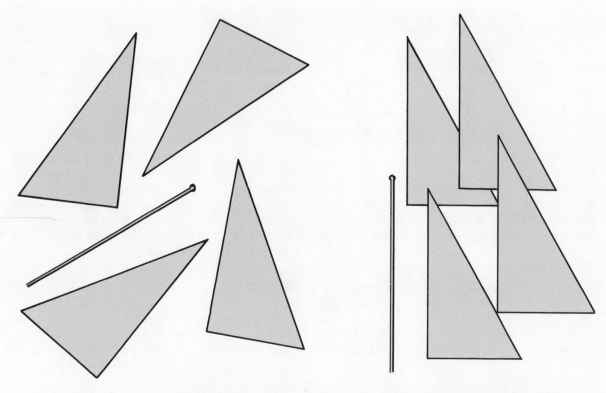

Fig. 3-9. Unity is what makes different elements look like they belong together. The pile of elements at left has no meaning. But if you placed them in order they suggest something.

Fig. 3-10. Rhythm repeats a certain form or pattern. Its purpose is to move the eye in the direction the designer wants it to go.

ROMAN TYPE

All Roman typefaces have light and heavy elements. They also have serifs. It is the differences in these light and heavy elements and the serif structure that places Roman type into its three categories.

OLD STYLE

The name, "Old style," refers to the shape of the letters. Old style letters seem to be informal as

though they were hand drawn. They are designed to look like the first Roman letters that appeared in print. The characters were originally formed by scribes using reed pens. The serifs are heavy.

MODERN

Modern typefaces show the influence of mechanical precision. There is a marked contrast between the elements of the letters. Modern Roman was introduced by an Italian printer, Bodoni, about 1760.

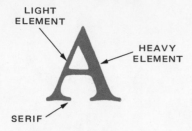

LIGHT ELEMENT

HEAVY ELEMENT

SERIF

Fig. 3-11. Parts of a typeface have names.

TRANSITIONAL ROMAN

Transistional typefaces have characteristics of both Old style and Modern. The contrast between thick and thin strokes is not so great as in Modern type. Serifs are long and have smooth, rounded curves.

TEXT TYPE

Text faces began with angular letter forms of medieval scribes. Johann Gutenberg chose this style. Text is used a great deal in church printing. It is difficult to read and should never be set in all capitals.

SQUARE SERIF

In square serif letters, all strokes are of the same weight. Even the serifs are just as heavy as the strokes of the letters. This face is used often for advertising.

SANS SERIF

Sans serif letters have no serifs at all. There is little or no change in the weight of the strokes of the letters. Compositors once argued that such faces are more difficult to read. However, they have become very popular not only in advertising but in magazines and textbooks. Sans serif is well suited for use where type is reversed. Refer again to Fig. 3-12.

SCRIPT

Script types look like handwriting. Four styles are shown in Fig. 3-12. Script types should never be set in all capitals. They would be very difficult to read.

OLD STYLE ROMAN

the Best Class

MODERN ROMAN WITH ITALICS

THIS TYPE FACE
ABCDEFabcdef

TRANSITIONAL ROMAN

ALL SIZES CARR
ied from 6 to 36-Pt.

TEXT

Must Have It
ABCDEFabcdefghi 123

SQUARE SERIF WITH ITALICS

ABCDEF abcdefgh
ABCDEFabcde

SANS SERIF WITH REVERSE

ABCDEFGHIJ klmnop
ABCDEFGHIJ klmnop

SCRIPT

Modern Alphabets
Advertising Letter,
This Versatile Face
The Trend in Fine Work

DECORATIVE

ABCDEFGHabcde
ART SHADOW
DESIGNED LETTER

Fig. 3-12. Examples of different type styles.

DECORATIVE

The name decorative is given to type that is designed for special or decorative purposes. Many different typefaces fit into this classification.

ITALICS

Many typefaces have, besides the regular vertical letters, a font of letters that lean to the right. Such type is called italic. It is often used for emphasis.

HOW TYPE IS PURCHASED

Hot type is purchased in fonts. A font contains an assortment of characters of one face in one size and in one style. It will have more of the letters most used (e, t, o and a) and fewer of less-used letters (k, x and z). A series of type includes several fonts of one typeface in different sizes such as 10, 12, 14, 18 and 24 point.

A collection of the various sizes and styles of one design of type is called a type family. An example is: Goudy Old style, Goudy Bold and Goudy Italic.

TYPE SELECTION

There are three important considerations when selecting type for a printing job:

1. Is the type easy to read? This quality is called legibility.
2. Is the type appropriate for the job at hand?
3. Do the typefaces chosen for the job go well together: This is called type harmony.

TYPE LEGIBILITY

The designer should always select a typeface that is easy to read. However, even very legible type may be set in a way that could make it hard to read. Examples of this are shown in Figs. 3-13 and 3-14.

Another factor that affects legibility is the space or leading placed between the lines. The longer the

Principles of design are used to place elements of graphic arts on a page. This is called the layout stage. The designer begins to put down	these elements by sketching them quickly, Fig. 5-11. These small, scaled-down drawings are called "thumbnail sketches."	They do not show much detail but give a general idea how the finished product will look. The designer may make a number of these and then select

Fig. 3-14. These columns are set too narrow. They, too, are hard to read.

line, the more leading it requires. In a commercial shop, leading is added in one of two ways.

1. Thin strips of lead are inserted between the lines.
2. In lead casting machines, the type is cast on larger slugs than indicated by the point size. For example, 10 point type may be cast on a 12 point slug.

Leading is not the same thing as letter spacing. Letter spacing is putting white space between letters. Capital letters may be spaced with good effect in display faces. However, lower case letters become less readable when letter is spaced. They should not be spaced except to justify lines of type matter.

PICKING THE RIGHT TYPE

Type should be suited to the message and the product. For example, an ad for lingerie needs a delicate typeface such as script. A headline for a plumbing catalog would look more appropriate in a heavy sans serif or square serif face.

When more than one face of type is to be used in a layout, the designer must select faces that go well together. Beginners should stick to the same family or families of type, or should use no more than two different styles of type until they are experienced.

LAYOUT

The layout is a plan for the printed piece. Layout work in the printing industry has three stages:

Principles of design are used to place elements of graphic arts on a page. This is called the layout stage. The designer begins to put down these elements by sketching them quickly, Fig. 5-11. These small, scaled-down drawings are called "thumbnail sketches." They do not show much detail but give a general idea how the finished product will look. The designer may make a number of these and then select one for the final layout.

Fig. 3-13. These lines are hard to read because they are too long. The eye tires from traveling too far across the page.

1. Thumbnail sketches.
2. Rough layout.
3. Comprehensive layout.

THUMBNAILS

Thumbnails are small drawings to show the relationships of the main elements of the proposed printed job. Sketching several ideas will help the printer and the customer decide which of these several ideas will be most suitable. All main elements should be included in the thumbnail: pictures, headings, trademarks, and the area taken up by the body of type. Fig. 3-15 shows some thumbnail sketches. One job may take only a few thumbnail sketches; another may take many. Designers will do several so that the client will have more choices.

ROUGHS

The rough layout is usually drawn full size so that it is easier to see the relationship of all the elements.

Fig. 3-15. Thumbnail sketches of a concert program give a miniature sized, rough idea of a layout.

Fig. 3-16. Rough layout gives idea of size and position of all elements.

Space requirements are also easier to determine. While the rough is not a work of art, it should be more carefully drawn than the thumbnails. Fig. 3-16 shows an example.

COMPREHENSIVE LAYOUT

The comprehensive or finished layout becomes the "working drawing" for the printer. It is to the printshop what the blueprint is to the building contractor.

The comprehensive layout is developed from the rough. It should be drawn up after the copy or information is decided upon.

The copy should be checked for correct spelling, accuracy, good grammar and punctuation. To save time and money, corrections should be made in the copy before it is set. Changes, other than those required to correct typesetters' mistakes, are billed to the customer.

The designer will also decide on the kind and color of paper, kind and color of ink and the size and style

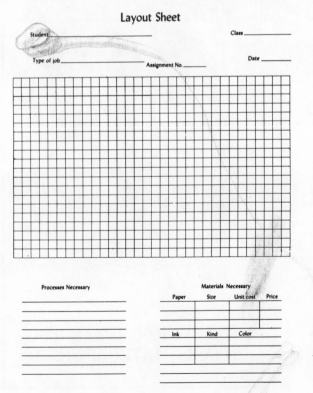

Fig. 3-17. This layout sheet is designed to handle school printing jobs. Note the space provided for other information.

Fig. 3-18. Finished layout.

of type. To make such decisions he or she should understand how the printed piece is going to be used.

The final layout should be drawn on a sheet of paper larger than the finished job, Fig. 3-17. This will allow room for directions in the margin. In this layout, the main lines of type can be lettered in or traced to look like the type being used. Illustrations are roughly shown in actual size. Small type in paragraph form is usually represented by lines. The copy is usually typed on a separate sheet and keyed to the proper space on the layout.

Fig. 3-18 shows the finished layout for a printing job. A folded sample is provided for jobs requiring more than one page. The sample is called a dummy. It should indicate copy position on both sides.

A mechanical is a finished, camera-ready layout. It is used when the printer plans to use the offset printing process or when an engraving is being made for letterpress. The mechanical is discussed in Unit 6.

MARKUP

Besides the comprehensive layout, a set of directions are needed. The directions tell how to set the type. The directions are called type specifications. The writing of specifications is called markup.

Printing buyers, layout artists and printers use special terms to describe type composition wanted. The terms are usually abbreviated. Fig. 3-19 shows a layout with specifications. They give the following information:

1. Type size and spacing between lines (leading). This is written in a double number such as 10/12. The first number is the point size and the second

36 pt Bookman Italic fl ℒ, Caps & lc on 22 picas —

48 pt "   "   " " " " " " " —

36   "   "   " " " " " " " ←

Posterization Photo —

18 pt Bookman Caps. fl ℒ on 22 picas —

Space as per layout

Fig. 3-19. Layout is marked up with specifications.

number is the type point size plus 2 points of leading between lines. Thus, 10/12 means "10 pt. type on a 12 pt. body." Each line of type will take up 12 points of space even though the type takes up only 10 points.

2. Type family and family branch. This is the name of the specific type family and branch of the type to be used.

3. Composition. This indicates, in abbreviated form, the combination of letters to be used. You will need to learn the following abbreviations:

caps — set in all caps

lc — set in lower case

clc — set in capitals and lower case

sc — set in small caps

4. Use of space or placement of lines. Again symbols or abbreviations are used:

fl l — set flush left

fl r — set flush right

ctr — center the line or lines

l — indent the line (number indicates how much)

just — make line flush right and left

5. Line width. This tells how wide the job should be set. It is expressed in picas or inches.

COPYFITTING

Copyfitting is the measuring of the space allowed in the design to see how much type can be set in that space. Another method is to prepare the copy first. Then the layout person will determine the space

Fig. 3-20. Ornaments can be purchased as a ready source of art. They can be enlarged, pasted to camera-ready layout as is or cast into metal.

needed. Unit 12, Mathematics for Printers, explains this procedure.

ART SOURCES

One source of art work is to have an artist produce it. But this material, in the form of line illustrations, decorations, borders and photos, can also be purchased from commercial sources.

Type ornaments, Fig. 3-20, are designs and illustrations cast in metal. Mounted type-high, they can be locked up in the typeform the same as type.

Clip art is printed, camera-ready material which is purchased in sheets or books. The layout artist cuts it off the sheet and fastens it to the layout. Fig. 3-21 shows typical clip art.

Fig. 3-21. Examples of clip art.

Tints, textures and backgrounds, Fig. 3-22, are other art materials readily available. Many of these materials are adhesive backed and require no wax or cement to attach them to a layout.

QUIZ — UNIT 3

1. What are design elements? Name five of them.
2. Proportion is one of the design elements. True or False?
3. The lighter lines in a typeface are called _____ _____; crosslines at the end of the elements are called _____.
4. All Roman typefaces have _____ and _____ elements and all have _____.
5. Small sketches that show the relationship of main elements in a layout are called:
   a. Comprehensive or finished layout.
   b. Design elements.
   c. Rough.
   d. Thumbnails.
   e. Mechanicals.
6. The abbreviation "fl l" means "set copy _____ _____."

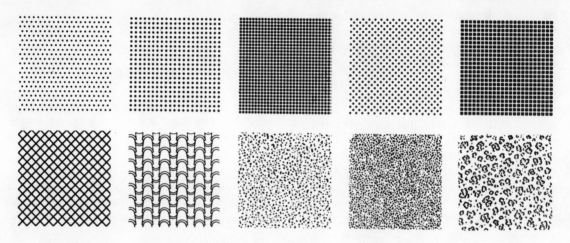

Fig. 3-22. Various screens can be purchased as background which adds interest and texture to a layout.

GENERATING TYPE

1. What are the methods of setting type and how is it done?
 a. Metal composition.
 b. Strike-on composition.
 c. Dry transfer.
 d. Photocomposition.
 e. Digital composition.

In the graphic arts, image and type generation are terms used for the process of producing words for the printed page. Other terms you will hear used for this process are type composition and typography. The people working in this area are called compositors or typographers.

The method of composing type has changed greatly in the last 10 years. New machines, new techniques, and new materials have enabled compositors to produce better quality work in a shorter time.

EARLY TECHNIQUES

In the very early days of printing, the person wanting to produce multiple copies of a message would carve the words into a block of wood. The letters would have to be in reverse, the block inked, and then pressed against each sheet of paper.

The first significant improvement over wood blocks was the casting of individual letters out of metal. These letters could be assembled into words and then printed. The letters, called type, were stored in boxes so they could be reassembled for a new message. Johan Guttenberg is given credit for this invention in A.D. 1450. This process improved the printing industry and allowed more people to have access to learning.

MACHINE SETTING OF METAL TYPE

While metal type has become a less popular method of setting type, there still is a great deal of it being done. If metal type is called for, it is usually done by machine.

LINECASTING MACHINES

Most machine set type is cast in lead using the Linotype, or Intertype, Fig. 4-1. They are similar in construction and operation.

Both cast complete line slugs from matrices. A matrix is a piece of brass or bronze into which the shape of the type is formed as a depression. When keys are pressed on the keyboard, the matrices drop in front of an opening to form a mold. Molten metal is forced into the mold. A solid slug (piece of type metal) is cast which bears a line of raised letters suitable for printing. The term ''hot type'' is normally given to type which is cast out of molten metal. After casting, the machine returns the matrices to storage.

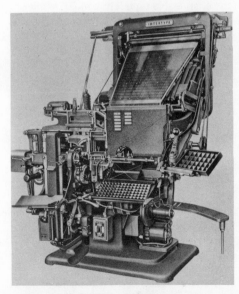

Fig. 4-1. Intertype slugcasting machine.

Fig. 4-2. Left. Monotype keyboard unit. Right. Casting unit. (Lanston Monotype Co.)

The slugs are assembled by hand into typeforms that can be used in printing. They are either placed on a press or used to make camera-ready proofs. Camera-ready means all elements are in place except photographs which must be screened. After serving their purpose, the slugs can be remelted.

Other machines used for metal typesetting are the Monotype machine, Fig. 4-2, and the Ludlow, Fig. 4-3.

STRIKE ON OR IMPACT TYPESETTERS

Many printing shops use the newer electric and electronic typewriters to produce camera ready copy.

One popular machine is the IBM typewriter, Fig. 4-4, with the changeable type font ball. This unit provides a variety of type faces. Fig. 4-5 shows the changing

Fig. 4-4. Office typewriters are often used to prepare strike-on copy. (IBM)

of the type font ball. Fig. 4-6 is a close-up of the ball unit.

Another popular typewriter for preparing copy uses a "daisy wheel" type font, Fig. 4-7. Fig. 4-8 shows

Fig. 4-3. Ludlow caster with matrix case. (Ludlow Typegraphic Co.)

Fig. 4-5. Changing the typeface on this machine requires only a few seconds to replace a ball-shaped type font. The ball clamps onto a shaft where it rotates and pivots to strike the right character on the paper.

Fig. 4-6. Font ball has four rows of characters circling the ball.

HEADLINE PHOTOTYPESETTERS

Single lines of type such as those used for headlines or posters can be set on a machine called a headliner. Very popular at one time, they have found less use since the phototypesetters of today can turn out type of all sizes.

Headliners are primarily used in schools and small print shops. One such machine is called the "strip printer," Fig. 4-9. The operator slides a negative strip of letters over photographically sensitive paper, Fig. 4-10. Each letter is exposed and the paper developed to make a finished copy, Fig. 4-11. This copy can now be pasted in position as camera-ready copy.

Fig. 4-7. This typewriter uses a "daisy wheel" type font.

Fig. 4-9. A strip printer makes contact print of type from piece of negative film.

a close-up of the "daisy wheel" unit out of the typewriter. The quality of type produced by these typewriters depends on the quality of ribbon used. A carbon ribbon for one-time use only will give the best print.

Fig. 4-10. Operator positions negative over photosensitive paper. Light above left hand exposes the paper.

Fig. 4-8. Characters are on tiny arms which circle a central core.

Fig. 4-11. Sensitized paper after exposure and development. Exposed parts turn black, forming the letters.

DRY TRANSFER TYPESETTING

Dry transfer type comes attached to font sheets, Fig. 4-12. Light blue lines traced on the layout sheet guide the artist or layout person in positioning the type of the sheet. Burnishing, a rubbing process, transfers the letters from the font sheet to the layout, Fig. 4-13. This process is used only for display lines, headlines, and for single words. Type from font sheets can be used only once.

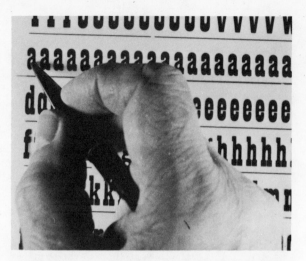

Fig. 4-12. Dry transfer type is attached to large sheets ready for use. (Pressure Graphics, Inc.)

PHOTO AND DIGITAL TYPESETTING

The majority of the graphic arts companies composing type today are using equipment that sets type photographically or digitally. These two types of machines look the same. The difference is in how the machine forms the letters when the operator strikes the keyboard. In both systems, the letters are formed on light sensitive paper which must be processed.

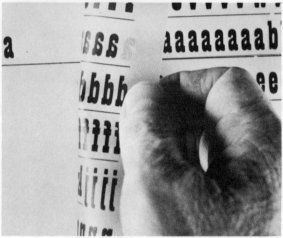

Fig. 4-13. Rubbing detaches dry transfer letters from the sheet and causes them to stick to the layout sheet.

Fig. 4-14. This compositor is setting type using a Compugraphic typesetter. The keyboard is used to enter letters on the display screen.

PHOTOTYPESETTING

A popular phototypesetting machine is the Compugraphic system, Fig. 4-14. This unit can have a number of input stations (keyboards). These multiple stations use a common output unit which sets the type on the photographic paper.

The letters are first formed on a display screen using a keyboard, then put into magnetic storage, Fig. 4-15. After the job is set and corrected, the operator calls for a printout. A light is projected through a negative to form a letter on the photographic paper. In some machines the negatives of the letters are on a strip that rotates and the light flashes as the proper letter passes, Fig. 4-16. Other manufacturers use a circular type font that rotates, Fig. 4-17. Both of these machines produce excellent quality type. The operator loads the output unit with the photographic paper in a light-tight box. The paper is fed through the machine line by line until the job is completed. The paper is removed from the typesetter in a special light-tight cassette, Fig. 4-18. The exposed paper is then fed through a procesor, Fig. 4-19. This machine

Fig. 4-17. Type font for photocomposition machine is contained on this disk.

Fig. 4-18. Box of exposed photographic paper is unloaded from photocomposition unit.

Fig. 4-15. Information entered into the typesetting system is stored on floppy disk. Magnetic particles on the surface of the disk hold the data.

Fig. 4-16. Negative type font strip. Light passes through letters on strip onto photographic paper.

Fig. 4-19. Photographic paper exposed in photocomposition unit is developed by a processor unit.

develops, fixes, and drys the paper so it can be placed on the paste-up board as camera-ready copy.

DIGITAL TYPESETTING

Digital typesetters, Fig. 4-20 and Fig. 4-21, look very much like phototypesetters. In these machines the letters are formed by a beam of light directed by magnetic impulses. Many of these machines use a laser light as the exposing device. The output looks the same as the work turned out on the phototype machine. The advantages of the digital typesetter include quicker output and less chance of dirt getting on the negative letter images.

PREVIEW SCREEN

A preview screen is used by some companies to electronically convert the various elements of the typeset material into position as it will appear in the final job, Fig. 4-22. This process is called WYSIWYG

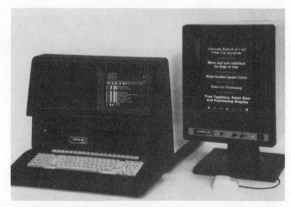

Fig. 4-20. Digital typesetter. Note the different font styles on the same screen.

Fig. 4-21. This digital typesetter allows layout to be done on the screen. The light blocked areas will contain pictures.

Fig. 4-22. A preview screen allows type composition and layout to be done electronically.

Fig. 4-23. Completed layout from processor after using preview screen to position elements.

(what you see is what you get). This operation requires special computer software programs. Considerable time is saved in the paste-up stage because the positioning is already done. Fig. 4-23 shows a job, produced by a preview screen, with the elements in position.

DIRECT INPUT TYPESETTER

A small number of shops are using direct input phototypesetters, Fig. 4-24. These machines set type directly to the photographic paper from the keyboard.

TYPESETTING WITH A PERSONAL COMPUTER

Personal computers (PC) with word processing capabilities are now being used in graphic arts. The words are set on a PC display screen and then stored on floppy disk. The copy is then transferred from the disk to the typesetter.

Fig. 4-24. Stand-alone direct typesetter.

Fig. 4-26. IBM personal computer.

DESKTOP PUBLISHING

Recent advances in computer software now permit typesetting and line art to be positioned for printing on personal computers such as the Macintosh, Fig. 4-25, and the IBM PC, Fig. 4-26. The term "desktop publishing" is given to this practice because both the computer and the laser printer (to produce camera ready output) will fit on a normal desktop.

Fig. 4-27 shows a page of a newsletter on the screen of a Macintosh computer. The pagination program draws information that was composed from a word processing program and a drawing software pro-

Fig. 4-27. A layout for a newsletter is being done on the screen. Both line art and type composition can be produced on the same layout screen.

Fig. 4-25. Macintosh personal computer.

gram. After the page meets with the operator's approval, it is sent to the printer for hard copy output. Fig. 4-28 shows the finished page produced by a laser printer now ready for paste up.

Many schools already have computers available. These can serve as basic typesetting machines for the graphic arts program. The fundamentals of typesetting using personal computers also apply to the complex typesetting equipment used by the graphic arts industry.

Fig. 4-28. Laser printer. A laser beam is used for image transfer. Note camera ready output at left. (Apple Computer, Inc.)

THE POINT SYSTEM

All methods of generating type images use the same measuring system for type. This is called the point system. A point is equal to 1/72 of an inch. Twelve points equal one pica and six picas equal one inch. Type, length of lines of type, and the height of columns are measured in picas and points. Fig. 4-29 shows a piece of type being measured.

The common measuring tool for the graphic arts is the printers' rule or line gauge, Fig. 4-30. One side of the rule is in inches. The other side is marked in picas and one-half picas (6 points). Type size is always given in points. Common sizes are illustrated in Fig. 4-31.

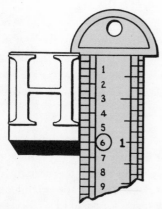

Fig. 4-29. Foundry type is measured from the nick side of the body to the back. The letter itself may be smaller than the body. This piece of type is 72 point (6 x 12).

Fig. 4-30. Printers' rule or line gauge. (H.B. Rouse)

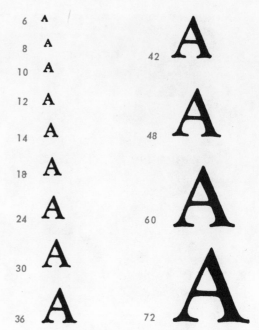

Fig. 4-31. Comparison of type sizes from 6 point to 72 point.

When the United States becomes metric, phototypesetting will convert to millimeters. Hot type probably will not drop the point system of type sizes. Type height, 0.9186 in., will convert to 23.32 mm. (There are 25.4 mm to an in.) For cold type, a metric unit called the "d" has been proposed. A "d" would equal 0.10 mm. Type size would be given in pairs of numbers representing tenths of millimeters. Thus, 40/60 would mean that the main stroke (body) of the type letter measures 4 mm high and the spacing is 6 mm.

SPACING MATERIAL

In foundry (or metal) type, words in a line are separated by pieces of metal called spaces. They are shorter than the type and have no characters on them. Spaces are also used to indent for paragraphs.

The unit of spacing is the em. It is the square of any size type. Spaces as wide or wider than an em are called quads. An em quad is a space which is square, see Fig. 4-32. All typesetting systems use this spacing including phototype and digital typesetting machines.

LEADS AND SLUGS

The term leading refers to space between lines. In metal type composition space is added by inserting

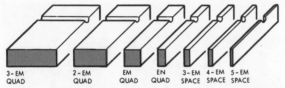

Fig. 4-32. Quads and spaces. A 3-em space is normally used between words.

metal strips, Fig. 4-33. The thickness of these strips is given in points. Leads are less than six points. Slugs are strips six points or thicker. Here again this terminology for spacing between lines on other typesetting processes is the same.

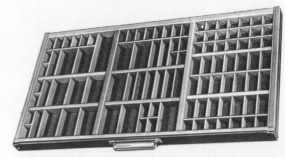

Fig. 4-33. Leads and slugs add space between lines of metal type composition. Most commonly used are 2 point leads and 6 point slugs.

SETTING TYPE BY HAND

Because most of the basic fundamentals of type and typesetting are learned by the hand set method, we suggest you set some type by this method.

STORING TYPE

All typesetting methods require a place to store the letters so they can be used over and over again. Foundry type or hand set type is placed in a shallow tray called a typecase. This case, Fig. 4-34, is divided into compartments. Each letter or character is assigned a compartment. Other characters also stored in the case include: numbers, punctuation marks, ligatures, spaces, and special characters such as the dollar sign, ampersand, and parentheses marks. Fig. 4-35 shows

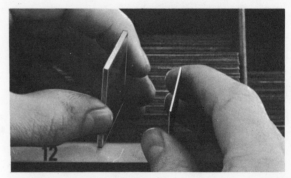

Fig. 4-34. A type case is divided into compartments to store different type.

the most common type case, the California job case.

Ligatures are letter combinations such as ff, fi, fl, ffi, and ffl, which are cast on a single body. These are made to protect the overhanging element of these letters. The overhanging part is called kerning, Fig. 4-36.

ffi	fl	5 em	4 em	' —	k	
j	b	c	d		e	
?						
!	l	m	n		h	
z						
x	v	u	t		3 em sp.	
q						

1	2	3	4	5	6	7	8
						ff	9
i		s		f	g		
						fi	0
o	y	p	w		,	en qd.	em qd.
				;	:	2&3	
a	r			.	'	em qd.	

$	—					
A	B	C	D	E	F	G
H	I	K	L	M	N	O
P	Q	R	S	T	V	W
X	Y	Z	J	U	&	ffl

Fig. 4-35. How type storage is organized by the California job case. Note that capital letters are stored separately.

Fig. 4-36. Ligatures and kerned letters are found only in foundry type.

COMPOSING STICK

The composing stick, Fig. 4-37, holds the type as it is assembled. Composing sticks come in several lengths according to the job being set.

SETTING TYPE

Before beginning to set foundry type, the measure or length of line must be determined. In the following

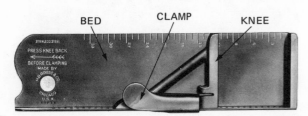

Fig. 4-37. Parts of a composing stick.   (H.B. Rouse)

assignment, you are given a measure. As you gain experience, you may choose the measure yourself.

Set the following copy (using a 10 or 12 point type):

eeeeeeeeee
aaaaaaaaaa
tttttttttt
eat eat eat eat

Proceed as follows:

1. Set the stick at a 15 pica measure.
2. Grasp the stick with the left hand tilting the open edge upward so pieces of type will not fall out.
3. Place a slug 15 pica long in the stick.
4. Pick letters from the typecase using the thumb and forefinger of the right hand.
5. Place them in the stick starting against the knee. Nicks must face upward toward thumb of your left hand. See Fig. 4-38. Steady the pieces in the stick with your left thumb.

Fig. 4-38. Set type in stick from left to right.

READING TYPE

The type you are setting will read from left to right but upside down and backward. With practice, you will soon be able to easily read type in this position. Try reading the single line of type in Fig. 4-39. Beware of type demons. These are certain letters, Fig. 4-40, which are easily mistaken for one another. Letters n

Fig. 4-39. Type is read from left to right and upside down.

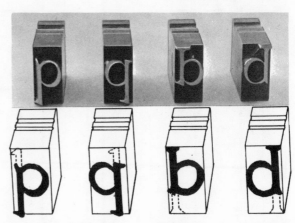

Fig. 4-40. Type demons are letters often mistaken for one another. Some are shown here. Left to right, b, d, p and q. Make sure nicks are up as you "read" them.

and u are also commonly confused. With nicks facing up the n looks like a u and vice-versa.

After you have placed 10 letters in the stick, fill out the line with as many quads as will fit. Then insert small spaces next to the type until the line fits firmly in the stick. Push the line away from the edge of the bed. If the type does not go beyond the edge, the line is justified (filled out) properly.

Set the rest of the lines using slugs as spacers. When finished, your stick should look like the one in Fig. 4-41.

Fig. 4-42. Method of transferring type from stick to galley. Top. Lift type from stick carefully as shown. Bottom. Place type in corner of galley.

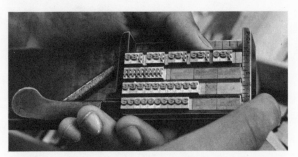

Fig. 4-41. Type is set and justified in the composing stick.

DUMPING THE STICK

Transfer of type to a gallery (three-sided metal tray) must be done carefully to avoid pied (spilled) type. Be sure there is a long slug along both sides of the type. Grasp the lines between thumbs and forefingers as shown in Fig. 4-42. Use second fingers as stops to prevent pieces of type from falling off the ends.

TYING THE TYPEFORM

With the type moved into a corner of the gallery, it is ready to be tied. The string must be long enough to go around the typeform four or five times. Starting in an open corner, wrap clockwise around the form. Overlap previous wrapping. Tuck remaining short length of string through the wrappings just around a corner, Fig. 4-43. Leave a loop below the wrappings and the end of the string above.

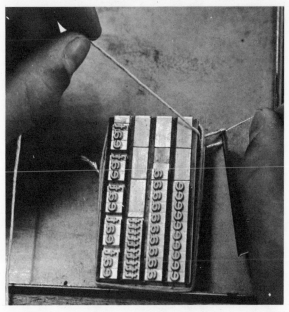

Fig. 4-43. Use a makeup rule to push loop of string under windings to tie it. It is then ready to use in making a proof.

PULLING A PROOF

Making a single copy of metal type is called "pulling a proof." This is done for several reasons.

1. It allows the matter to be proofread for errors. (This is called "proofreading.")

2. It is an exact copy of the type matter and can be used in making a dummy or camera-ready layout for the printer. (A dummy is a rough copy of the finished layout which the printer can use to arrange hot type in a chase. A camera-ready layout is a pasteup of type and illustrations ready to be reproduced on film.)

Proofs can be pulled with hand equipment or with a proof press. See Fig. 4-44.

To pull a proof, place the gallery and typeform on the bed of the proof press. Put a small amount of ink on the ink plate. Roll it out to a thin film with a small roller (brayer). Refer again to Fig. 4-44. Carefully roll the brayer across the typeform to ink the type. Place a sheet of paper over the type. Do not drag the paper across the inked form.

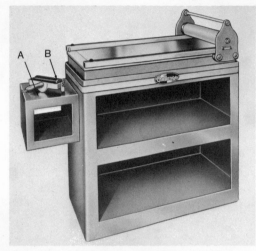

Fig. 4-44. Proof press makes single copies of type matter. A— Ink plate. B—Brayer. (Challenge Machinery Co.)

Roll the press cylinder across the form. Grasp a corner or edge of the sheet and lift it slowly from the form. This is your completed proof. Be careful not to brush your hands over it while the ink is still wet. It will smear.

PROOFREADING

Before printing, type has to be carefully read and corrected. This examination will show up misspellings, omitted words and other problems. Larger shops employ proofreaders. They read the type-set material and make corrections on the proof so the compositor knows what to do to fix it. See Fig. 4-45. In the school shop, each student corrects his or her own proof and then has it checked by the instructor. The corrections must be reset by the typesetter and the corrections placed in the copy. The proofreader must never assume that the reset copy is correct. It, too, is reread to catch additional errors.

It is not enough to simply read over the proof. It must be compared sentence by sentence with the

Fig. 4-45. Proofreaders work in pairs, one following the original copy and one correcting proof.

original copy. Use a pencil and mark the proof for corrections using the standard proofreading marks as shown in Fig. 4-46. Imagine a vertical line down through the center of your proof. Put the marks for the left half in the left margin and the marks for the right half in the right margin. Watch spelling, punctuation and word division. When in doubt, check with a dictionary or style manual.

SAMMY SAFETY SAYS:

"While working in a graphic art laboratory, you share in the responsibility for keeping a safe and orderly work area.

Here are some safe practices to be remembered. Other safety precautions will be brought to your attention as needed.

1. Ask your teacher to approve all work you plan to do.
2. Use good common sense. The laboratory is not a playground.
3. Read and pay attention to safety signs.
4. While working around a printing press, roll up your sleeves and remove your necktie. It is advisable to wear a shop apron.
5. Do not hold type in your mouth.
6. If you have any reason to believe that a machine is not safe, report the fact to your teacher immediately.
7. Never experiment with a machine or other print shop equipment you do not fully understand. Fingers or a hand in the wrong place can cause serious injury and/or crippling.

X	Defective letter		⊙	Colon	no ¶	No paragraph
	Push down space		;/	Semicolon	wf	Wrong font letter
	Turn over			Apostrophe	stet	Let it stand
	Take out (delete)			Quotation	tr	Transpose
∧	Insert at this point			Hyphen	caps	Capitals
✓✓	Space evenly		///	Straighten lines	SC	Small capitals
#	Insert space		⊏	Move over	l.c.	Lower-case letter
⌣	Less space		⊐	Em quad space	ital	Italic
⊂⊃	Close up entirely			One-em dash	Rom	Roman letter
⊙	Period			Two-em dash	(?)	Verify
⋀	Comma		ℋ	Make paragraph	Spell out	Spell out
lig	Ligature		bf	Bold face	out see copy	Out see copy

Fig. 4-46. Proofreaders' marks are a kind of shorthand that tells the printer what must be corrected.

8. Do not talk to a person operating a machine. Adjust machine only when power is off.
9. Put dirty rags used around the print shop in, not near, the can provided for the purpose. Keep the can covered.
10. Never use rags saturated with cleaning fluid near an open flame.
11. Wipe up spilled oil. Someone may slip on it.
12. Report accidents, no matter how minor, to your teacher or safety supervisor immediately.''

CORRECTING ERRORS

Most corrections can be made with the typeform in the galley. It is easier to work on a type bank (slanted work surface of a type cabinet). Untie the form. If the correction does not change the length of the line, you can lift the letter with a tweezers. Be careful not to damage the typeface.

If the correction changes the length of the line, place the line back in the composing stick. This is necessary to rejustify the line.

When corrections are completed, replace the line in the form, retie it and pull another proof. This is called a revised proof. If the form is to be placed on a press, store it until needed. If not, type can be redistributed.

DISTRIBUTING TYPE

Returning the pieces of type to the typecase is called type distribution. First take the galley of type to the bank. Untie the form and pick up one line of type at a time, Fig. 4-47. Using the right hand, return each

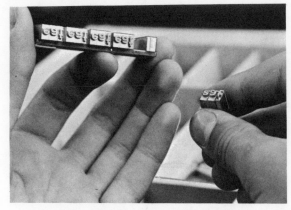

Fig. 4-47. Foundry type is returned to the case.

piece to the typecase. Spaces should be put aside in the galley. They are distributed to the typecase last.

SETTING TYPE BY COMPUTER

Modern graphic arts companies use computers to set type. Computer typesetting is faster than setting

SAMMY SAFETY SAYS:

''Only EPA approved cleaning fluids should be used to clean type. Rags saturated with fluid should be kept in a closed OSHA-approved metal container to prevent fire.''

type by hand or by machine. Linecasting machines are replaced by keyboards and digital typesetters. The quality of computer-set type is also better than the quality of hot type because the use of ink is eliminated.

Digital typesetting also surpasses phototypesetting. There are no mechanical image carriers. Instead of using negative font strips to produce images, digital typesetting systems use computer controlled lasers. The images are transferred to light-sensitive paper using an electronically controlled beam of light. The paper is then developed to produce the image.

COMPUTER WORKSTATION

The compositor works at a computer workstation. A typical workstation contains five parts: the computer, keyboard, display screen, data storage, and hardcopy unit, Fig. 4-48.

When the computer is turned on, it must first be programmed to understand typesetting commands. Special software is used to generate the type fonts needed by the compositor.

The words and characters are entered into the computer using the keyboard, Fig. 4-49. Special commands are entered to determine point size, leading, line width, and type font. The commands also direct the system to justify and hyphenate the type. When

the copy is printed, these commands will direct the digital typesetter on how to print the type.

The compositor views the entered data on the display screen. The display screen shows the words, characters, and typesetting commands. Commands are separated from the text by brackets, Fig. 4-50.

Fig. 4-49. The keyboard contains all the alphanumeric keys found on a typewriter (black keys) plus special function keys (white keys).

Fig. 4-48. There are five components of a computer typesetting workstation.

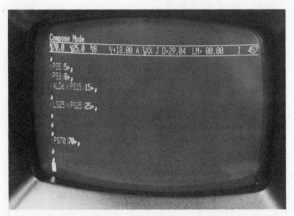

Fig. 4-50. The display screen has a parameter line (on top) to tell point size, font, leading, and line length. Commands to change the parameters are typed in brackets. This set of commands and characters produced the numbers in Fig. 4-52.

Misspelled words or other errors caught at this time can be easily corrected.

When a page of copy is finished, it is saved in permanent data storage. The most common method of storing information is a floppy disk, refer to Fig. 4-15.

After all the copy and commands are keyed in and stored in memory, a hardcopy print is produced on photographic paper. The paper is removed from the typesetter in a light-tight box and then placed in the processor, Fig. 4-51.

Fig. 4-51. Light-sensitive paper is taken from the digital typesetter and processed in a separate machine to develop the image.

Once the copy is through the processor, it is ready for layout as camera-ready copy, Fig. 4-52. The hardcopy output from the typesetter does not include the special commands seen on the screen. They only determined the size and font of the text.

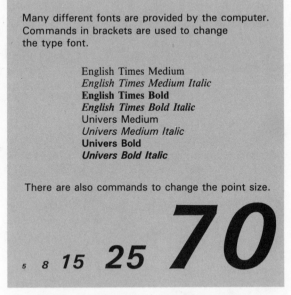

Fig. 4-52. This hardcopy output shows how different fonts and point sizes are easily produced by a digital typesetter.

QUIZ — UNIT 4

1. The Linotype and Intertype machines are examples of material casting machines. True or False?
2. In _____ composition, the image is made when the character strikes an inked or carbon ribbon.
3. Explain the principle of phototypesetting.
4. What does keyboarding mean?
5. Explain how type is set digitally.
6. List the methods of generating type.
7. A _____ is equal to 1/72 inch.
8. The basic unit for spacing of printed material is the _____.
9. Metal strips used to put space between lines are called:
   a. Leading and slugs.
   b. Spaces.
   c. Quads.
   d. 3-em spaces.
   e. Composing sticks.
10. Discuss the different storage methods for type.
11. The small rubber roller used to ink type for proofing is called a _____.

CONTINUOUS TONE COPY PREPARATION

UNIT 5

1. How the camera works.
2. Becoming familiar with photographic materials.
3. Learning to develop film.
4. Producing prints by contact and enlargment.

Many publications and graphic communication materials contain pictures to help carry a message to the reader. This unit will show how to make photographs to use in printing processes. Knowing the processes also makes us better buyers and consumers of photographic processes and materials.

Information in this unit will also help us to understand the photography used in graphic arts process camera work.

ELEMENTS OF PHOTOGRAPHY

Photography is the art or process of producing images on sensitized surfaces through controlled action of light. Elements necessary for producing a photograph are:

1. A camera, Fig. 5-1.
2. A light source, either the sun or artificial lights.
3. Sensitized materials (film and photographic paper).
4. Chemicals for developing the film and paper.
5. Devices to make the photographic prints (an enlarger or contact box).

THE CAMERA

A camera is a light-tight box. It holds the light-sensitive film, and controls the amount of light falling on the film. Even the simplest box camera has six basic parts:

1. Camera body. A light-proof box with a device to hold film at one end and an opening for a lens at the other end.
2. Lens. A specially shaped glass mounted in the

front of the camera body. It changes or focuses the rays of reflected light to form an image of the subject on the film.
3. Shutter. A movable metal leaf or cloth covering over the lens to keep out light. It opens for a fraction of a second to allow light to enter and expose the film.
4. Shutter release. A lever or plunger which trips the spring-loaded shutter.
5. View finder. A "window" which shows the operator what will be included in the picture.
6. Film advance. A lever or wheel to move the film after each exposure.

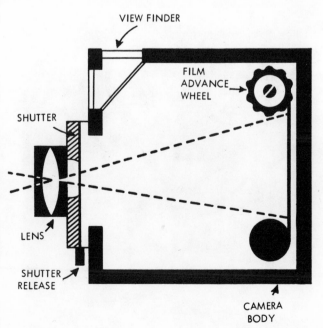

Fig. 5-1. Basic construction of simple box camera.

SPECIAL FEATURES

Better cameras have additional features that are important for proper exposure of the film:

1. Variable shutter speeds to control the length of time the shutter is open.
2. A device, Fig. 5-2, to change the size of the lens opening.

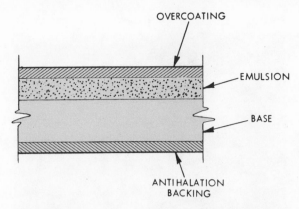

Fig. 5-4. Cross section of a piece of film showing all the layers. Emulsion layer contains light-sensitive silver halides.

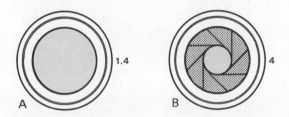

Fig. 5-2. Iris diaphragm is a series of overlapping leaves that can make the lens opening smaller or larger to let in different amounts of light. A—Diaphragm wide open to admit most light possible. B—Diaphragm partly closed to admit less light.

3. A focusing device to change the distance between the lens and film. It keeps the image sharp as distance changes.
4. A built-in light meter to tell the camera operator what combination of shutter speed, lens opening and film speed is correct for a good picture.

Cameras are designed in many different sizes and shapes, to allow them to do the many jobs they are called upon to perform. See Fig. 5-3.

FILM

Photographic film is made up of a ribbon of clear material — usually cellulose acetate — which is the base for several layers of other materials, Fig. 5-4.

One is a layer of light-sensitive gelatin holding fine grains called silver halides.

The action of light on silver halides is seen when the film is developed. Exposed silver halides change to metallic silver when film is soaked in developer. Unexposed halides get washed off by a fix or hypo solution. The image, called a negative, is a reverse of the picture taken. It is used to produce a picture on photographic paper. See Fig. 5-5.

FILM SPEED

Film is rated by an ASA number. The higher the number the more sensitive the film is to light. We say that sensitive film is "fast." This means less light is needed to get a good image. The ASA number is used to set the light meter if one is used.

PHOTOGRAPHIC PAPER

PHOTOGRAPHIC PAPER is light sensitive like film. Film is used to get the negative image. Paper produces the positive image when light is projected through the negative onto the paper.

Fig. 5-3. Popular small format cameras. Sizes indicate one dimension of the film frame. Left to right. Instamatic 110, 35 mm rangefinder type, 120 twin lens reflex, and 35 mm single lens reflex.

Fig. 5-5. Top. Negative shows light and dark areas in reverse. Light areas are where unexposed halides were washed off. Bottom. Positive contact print made from the negative.

Newspapers need to make prints in a hurry to meet their deadlines. They have turned to a very rapid method of making them on STABILIZATION papers. These papers have the developer mixed in the emulsion. The print is exposed exactly as other photographic papers, but a special processor develops it. See Fig. 5-6.

TAKING PHOTOGRAPHS

Load your camera with a roll of black and white film. You will need to take a series of pictures. If pictures are being taken outdoors in daylight you can estimate the exposure setting. Recommendations for shutter speed and aperture settings for sunny or overcast days are packed with the film. Where lighting is limited, a light meter measures the light and indicates best shutter speeds and lens openings, Fig. 5-7.

Fig. 5-6. Developing a stabilization print. Top. Exposed print is fed into the machine holding chemical bath. Bottom. Finished print takes about a minute to process.

Fig. 5-7. Setting and reading a typical light meter. A—Set indicator for emulsion speed of film. B—Press button to activate meter. C—Set pointer to match needle of meter, D. E—Select shutter speed and find closest f-stop. Set f-stop and shutter speed on camera.

DEVELOPING FILM

Photographic film is sensitive to all light. It must be handled in total darkness until it is in the light-tight developing tank.

Practice loading the tank under room light until you know the technique well enough to try it with the lights out. Follow these steps:

1. Transfer film to a developing tank, Fig. 5-8.
   a. Adjust the reel for the film size before turning out the light, Fig. 5-9.

Fig. 5-8. Parts of a light-tight film tank. Clockwise, assembled tank, agitator, cover, reel and open tank.

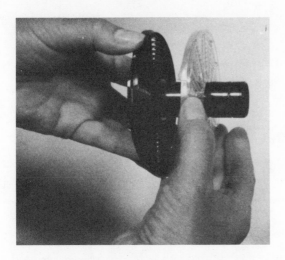

Fig. 5-9. One side of adjustable reel is movable and can be adjusted to different size film.

Fig. 5-10. Film is fed onto reel. Top. This type reel feeds from the outside in. Bottom. Stainless steel reels are loaded from the center.

b. With the lights out, remove the film from its cartridge or begin to unwind the paper on the spool until the beginning edge of the film can be felt.

c. Feed the film onto the reel, Fig. 5-10.

2. Place the loaded reel in the tank and attach cover securely.

3. Turn on the lights and proceed with the developing of the film.

4. Pour developer into the tank through the opening in the top, Fig. 5-11.

5. Vigorously rotate the reel counterclockwise a few times to remove air bubbles and assure even wetting of the emulsion.

6. Agitate for five seconds at 30-second intervals.

7. At end of development time, pour out the developer.

8. Rinse film in stop bath or water at 65 to 75 deg. F (18 to 24 deg. C) for specified time.

Fig. 5-11. Measured amount of developer is poured into developing tank. Short stop and fix are measured out in same way. Timer is necessary for determining length of time in each solution.

9. Pour out stop bath solution and pour in fixing bath or hypo. Fix 5 to 10 minutes with occasional agitation.

10. Then remove the cover and pour off the solution.

11. Wash film 20 to 30 minutes.

12. After washing, pour off a little water. Add a wetting agent to prevent water spotting of the film. Agitate for 5 seconds.

13. Hang up the film and allow to dry, Fig. 5-12.

Fig. 5-12. Attach clips at each end during drying.

PRINTMAKING

In the printmaking process, light is projected through the negative or negatives onto the photographic paper. Prints may be made either by contact method or by enlarging.

In contact printing, the negatives are placed on top of the photographic paper during the exposure. In enlarging, the film is at a distance from the photographic paper.

With small format negatives, contact printing is used only for making proofs. Prepare the negatives by cutting 35 mm and 110 film into strips of five frames each. Cut 120 film into strips of three frames. You are ready to make a contact print.

CONTACT PRINTMAKING

Turn out the room lights and perform all printmaking steps under an OC (greenish yellow) SAFE-LIGHT. A 1A (red) safelight is also suitable.

1. Center a sheet of normal contrast paper on the enlarger easel.
2. Arrange negatives on the paper, emulsion side down.
3. Cover negatives with a clear glass to hold them in contact with the paper as shown in Fig. 5-13.
4. Turn on the enlarger and make a 15-second exposure with the lens aperture closed down two stops from wide open or about f/8.
5. Develop the print.

DEVELOPING THE PRINT

Developing must also be carried on under safe-lights. The process is similar to developing film except that the chemicals are in open trays, Fig. 5-14.

The print is moved through the three baths, developer, stop bath and fix, following manufacturer's recommendations. Approximate time in each solution: developer, 45 to 90 seconds with tray agitation; stop bath, 10 to 15 seconds; fix, 5 to 7 minutes. After fixing, wash prints 30 to 45 minutes in

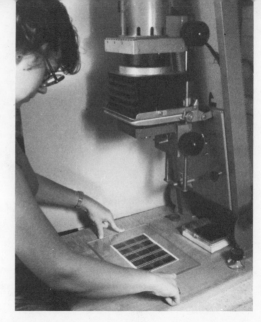

Fig. 5-13. Preparing to contact print. Negatives are placed on top of photographic paper. Light will be supplied by enlarger.

running water. Chemicals and wash water should be at or near 68 deg. F (20 deg. C).

Dry prints between blotters or in a print dryer. New resin coated papers are air dried.

Fig. 5-14. Three trays are needed for developing. Try always to arrange trays left to right: developer, stop bath and fix.

ENLARGING

Prints larger than negatives are called enlargements. An enlarger works as follows: Negative is placed in an enlarger. Light projects through negative onto a lens. The lens focuses the image on photographic paper placed on enlarger easel. See Fig. 5-15.

To make an enlargement:

1. Place negative in the carrier, Fig. 5-16.
2. Turn on the enlarger, open lens aperture. Adjust focus on the easel.
3. Stop lens down to aperture desired.
4. Turn off enlarger light.
5. Place photosensitive paper on the easel as shown in Fig. 5-17.
6. Expose for desired time. A timer turns off the light after the desired exposure.

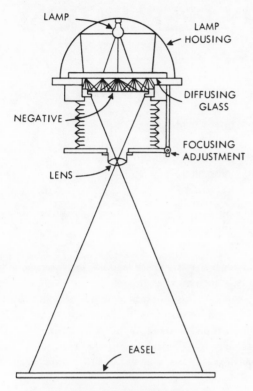

Fig. 5-15. Diagram of how an enlarger works.

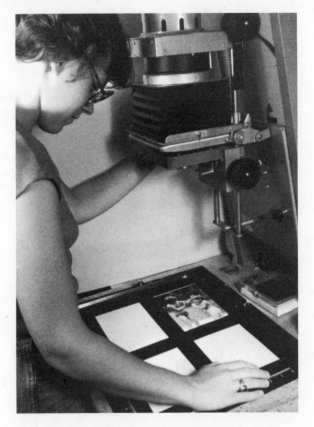

Fig. 5-17. Exposing the photographic paper.

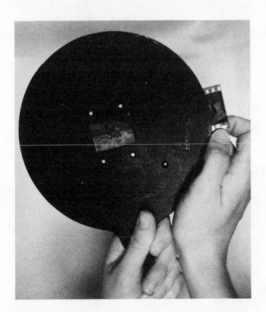

Fig. 5-16. Negative holder is a two-piece metal plate. It parts to receive film which must be centered in the window.

QUIZ – UNIT 5

1. Name five elements that are needed to make a photograph.

2. _____ _____, the light-sensitive material is held in the _____ layer.

3. The higher the ASA number of a film, the more sensitive it is to light. True or False?

4. The chemical bath which removes the unexposed silver halides from the film is called (check all that apply):
   a. Developer.
   b. Fix.
   c. Hypo.
   d. Stop bath.
   e. Wetting agent.

5. In the _____ process, the film is at a distance from the light-sensitive paper.

CAMERA-READY COPY PREPARATION

UNIT 6

1. Preparing a layout for the process camera.
2. Cropping and scaling of illustrations.
3. Preparing illustrations for overprints and reverses.

Pasteup is the stage in which copy elements — type, line art and photographs — are either fastened down on a heavy, white sheet or their position is marked to be stripped into the film later. It is also called camera-ready copy preparation.

EQUIPMENT AND MATERIALS

Equipment and materials needed for pasteup are simple and inexpensive, Fig. 6-1. Included are:

1. Drawing board. This should be flat and smooth with at least one edge true (straight).

2. Layout sheets. These should be a heavy white stock, such as index bristol.
3. T-square. This is used to draw level (horizontal) lines and for positioning all elements (type, art and photos) on the sheet.
4. Triangle. This is used with the T-square to draw vertical lines or align copy. Slanted lines can also be drawn.
5. Pencils and pens. Used for drawing lines, making freehand sketches and marking instructions. Instructions can be marked on the layout sheet in blue pencil. Since blue does not photograph, you will not need to erase them later.

Fig. 6-1. Layout tools and materials are assembled on the layout table. Can you name all of them?

6. Adhesive materials. Either rubber cement or wax can be used to attach copy elements to the layout sheet. Some graphic artists use double sided tape to hold copy in place. However, it is hard to work with and nearly impossible to remove without ruining the copy.
7. Rules, gages, compasses, cutting tools and masking film.

The finished layout is often called a "mechanical." It is ready to be converted into film on the process camera. All elements which will be printed as a solid line are present. Spaces are left where screened (halftone) illustrations will be stripped in later. The space is filled with a square of black paper or a red masking film. When photographed, it leaves a "window" or clear space in the negative. The screened negative is attached over the window later.

In relief printing, the pasteup stage of printing is not needed. The metal type, itself, is placed on the press along with the blocks of wood and metal which hold the line and halftone illustrations.

PASTEUP PROCEDURE

In preparation for making a pasteup, place a layout sheet on the drawing board. Use the T-square and triangle to position it squarely on the board. Fasten it down securely with drafting tape across the corners. Assemble copy elements and study the rough layout, Fig. 6-2.

Most layout sheets are already ruled to show the image area. All copy must be placed inside this area. If the sheet is not marked, rule it according to your instructor's guidance. Make all lines with a light blue pencil so the film will not reproduce them.

Trim proofs, allowing only a small margin of white around the type, Fig. 6-3. Spread rubber cement or

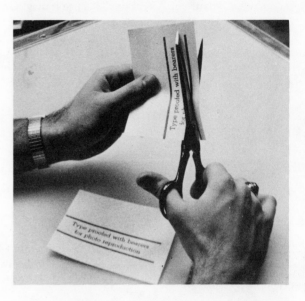

Fig. 6-3. Trimming away of bearer marks is done after adhesive has been applied to back.

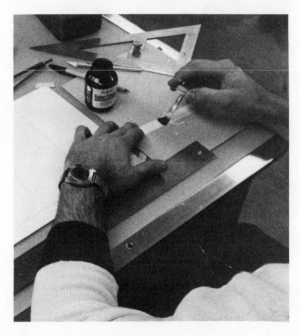

Fig. 6-4. Apply adhesive to back of copy elements. Work on a protective sheet of paper to keep adhesive off layout table.

Fig. 6-2. All elements — rough layout, type, illustrations and photographs — are inspected before pasteup.

wax on the backs of the sheets of type. See Figs. 6-4 and 6-5. If rubber cement is used, prepare only one proof at a time and attach the proof to the layout sheet while the cement is still wet. Use the T-square to align the type. Do not disturb the copy until the cement is dry.

Attach line art in the same manner. Alignment of art may be a matter of "eyeballing" it since it may be impossible to find a horizontal line to align with the T-square.

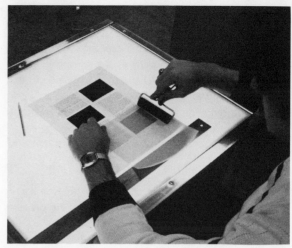

Fig. 6-6. Completed mechanical is rolled with plastic roller to adhere materials to the layout. Black squares are where halftones (photographs) will be placed later.

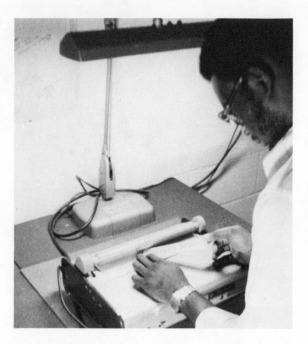

Fig. 6-5. Applying wax to a piece of copy.

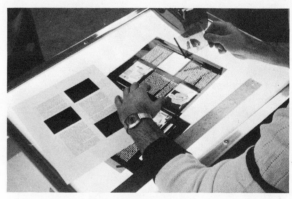

Fig. 6-7. Halftone film of photograph is stripped into the negative where the black squares appear in the mechanical.

When elements are attached to the layout sheet, carefully press down the material with a plastic roller, Fig. 6-6, to attach the material securely.

Because photographs have various shades of gray, they must be photographed separately through a halftone screen. Fig. 6-7 shows a halftone film ready to be attached to a film negative of the layout.

LAYOUT FOR ADDITIONAL COLOR

When more than one color will be used on a layout, a separate overlay or flap is attached to the layout for every color. Fig. 6-8 is a mechanical prepared for two colors.

The flaps are made on transparent sheets so that the graphic artist can see where to place the elements.

Fig. 6-8. A two-color layout. Register marks are the circles with crosses over them.

The first step in preparing an overlay is to attach the clear flap to the mechanical which is also called the key sheet. Then the elements in color are attached to the flap with rubber cement or wax. Black paper or red masking film can be used for solid color areas. If a pattern is required, this can be applied to the overlay. Some are shown in Fig. 6-9. This material is burnished (rubbed) in place and trimmed with a knife to the proper size. Adhesive-backed border materials, Fig. 6-10, are prepared in rolls. They are applied to a mechanical wherever a border is required, Fig. 6-11.

Fig. 6-11. Border tape is attached to mechanical.

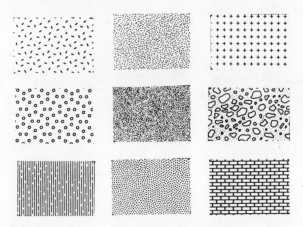

Fig. 6-9. Special patterns are available to add a design to layouts. This material is supplied on a clear, pressure-sensitive adhesive backing.

CROPPING PHOTOGRAPHS

Cropping a photograph is marking it so the printer will know what part of it is to be used. This must be done without marking up or damaging the picture. There are several ways to do this. One way is to place the crop marks on an overlay as in Fig. 6-12. Another cropping method is shown in Fig. 6-13.

Fig. 6-12. Crop marks placed on an overlay prevent damage to photograph.

If the photograph must be enlarged or reduced to fit the layout, it will be necessary to scale it. Scaling is determining the size of one dimension after the other dimension is changed. This dimension is found on the proportion scale, Fig. 6-14. Another method of scaling is the diagonal method shown in Fig. 6-15.

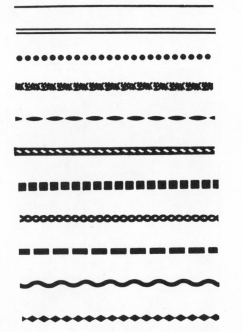

Fig. 6-10. These are samples of the adhesive-backed border materials available.

Fig. 6-13. Crop marks should be placed only in border of photo if overlay is not used. Use felt tip pen or grease pencil.

Fig. 6-14. Proportion scale is used to size illustrations. Find original size of one side of an illustration on the inner scale. Align it with the new size on outside scale. The new size of the other dimension will appear opposite the original size of the side. This scale is in metric.

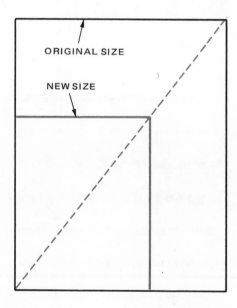

Fig. 6-15. Diagonal line drawn lightly on back of illustration will help find new size of illustration. Mark new size of illustration along bottom. Extend mark upward in a parallel line until it intersects. Point of intersection is new height.

RULING FORMS

Ruled lines can be drawn by the graphic artist with a T-square and a ruling pen. See Fig. 6-16. The lines could also be made by scratching away the emulsion of the film with a negative scribing tool.

OVERPRINTS AND REVERSES

Preparing a photograph for an overprint or reverse requires an overlay like the one used on a mechanical that is to be printed in two colors. Or, the overprint material could be produced photographically. See Fig. 6-17.

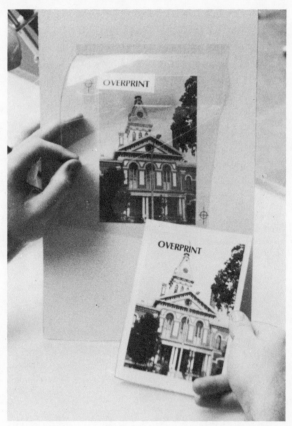

Fig. 6-17. Preparing a photograph for overprinting or reversing out of type. In upper illustration, type is placed on an overlay. In photo at bottom, two negatives — one of the type and one of the building — were used to make the photographic print.

Fig. 6-16. Proper technique for drawing ruled lines with pen and T-square.

QUIZ — UNIT 6

1. _____ is the stage in printing when copy elements are fastened to a mechanical.
2. Cropping of photos involves:
   a. Reducing the photograph to the right size.
   b. Marking the area to be used.
   c. Finding out the second dimension when the first has been enlarged or reduced.
3. Which of the following statements are correct? An overlay is used to:
   a. Carry crop marks for a photograph.
   b. Hold copy elements for a layout being printed in more than one color.
   c. Hold copy elements that must be overprinted on a photograph.
   d. All of the above.
   e. None of the above.

PHOTOCONVERSION

UNIT 7

1. Understanding the processes used in converting camera-ready copy to film.
2. Understanding the materials and equipment used in photoconversion.
3. Making conversions of line and continuous tone copy.
4. Principles of color separation, duotones, PMTs and posterization.

Some types of printing must use photography to produce image carriers. You will recall that an image carrier is the material that is placed in the press to receive the ink. It contains the message — words and pictures — that are to be printed. The image carrier is inked only in the message area and transfers this ink to the material being printed.

Copy, produced in the typesetting and pasteup stages, is photographed to get a negative. The process is called PHOTOCONVERSION. Copy ready to be photographed, you will recall, is called "camera-ready" copy. Two types of negatives are needed:

1. A line negative. This is a film of all images that print solid lines and shapes on the paper.
2. Screened or halftone negative. This is a film made of a photograph. The screening breaks the image up into a dot pattern.

The photography used to produce these negatives is very similar to the continuous tone photography discussed in Unit 5. The process requires a much larger camera with a special board to hold the material being photographed. Also needed is a CONTACT SCREEN which produces the dot pattern in the negative. This is a film with a grid pattern in it.

PROCESS CAMERA

The camera, called a process camera, is used only where printing materials are being photographed. There are two types:

1. Horizontal camera, Fig. 7-1, so called because line of sight is horizontal.
2. Vertical camera, Fig. 7-2, so called because line of exposure is vertical.

DARKROOM CAMERAS are designed to be used only in a darkroom. Sometimes only the case or film end is in the darkroom while the rest of the camera is in a lighted room.

Other cameras are designed to be used under normal room lights. They are called GALLERY CAMERAS and film must be loaded in a light-tight holder before it is placed in the film back.

PARTS OF A CAMERA

Referring again to Figs. 7-1 and 7-2, you can see that regardless of design, every process camera has the same essential parts:

1. A copyboard which holds the copy under glass while it is being photographed.
2. A film holder which supports the film, holding it perfectly flat during the exposure. It must be parallel to the lens board for sharp negatives.
3. A lens board which supports the lens, a shutter, shutter controls and aperture controls. Like a handheld camera, the process camera has a diaphragm which can be stopped down to allow less light to fall on the film. But the controls are more complex, Fig. 7-3.

If the idea of aperture openings is confusing, imagine that you are inside a box. If you make a hole in the box with a pin, a small amount of light is let in. This would be like the smallest aperture opening such as f/32. But if you were to make the hole bigger with a pencil, more light would come in. It would be comparable to opening the aperture to f/8. If the hole were enlarged still more, the opening might compare to an f/4 aperture.

By manually adjusting the aperture setting, the camera operator controls the amount of light

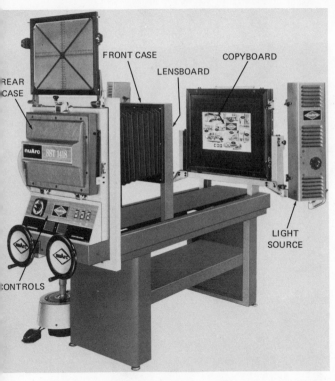

Fig. 7-1. All modern horizontal process cameras have some parts that are essential. This design is also called a gallery camera. Line of sight is horizontal.

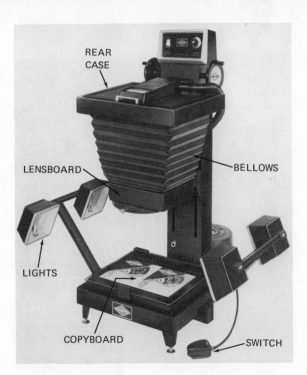

Fig. 7-2. Lens board and copyboard of vertical camera are in horizontal position. Line of sight is vertical.

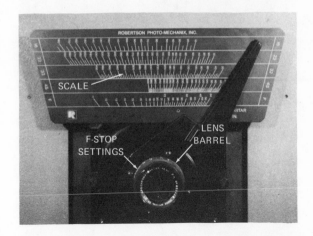

Fig. 7-3. Aperture is controlled by a long arm. Scale allows operator to adjust opening according to how much the copy is enlarged or reduced. Settings for f-stops are also marked on the lens barrel.

reaching the film from the copyboard. Fig. 7-4 shows the relationship of different lens openings.

4. Focus or scaling system. It adjusts the film plane, lens and copyboard for sharpness and correct sizing of the film. The film plane does not move but lens board and copyboard can be moved. The scales are marked in percentages. If the copy is to be 100 percent of original size (same size), both scales are set at 100, Fig. 7-5. This will produce a sharp focus and the correct size image on the film.

5. A light source and timer are needed to assure enough light to expose the film. The lights are attached to the camera frame, Fig. 7-6, and can be adjusted to change the angle at which the light strikes the copyboard. The timer, Fig. 7-7, is set by the operator. Then it will automatically shut off the lights and close the lens shutter.

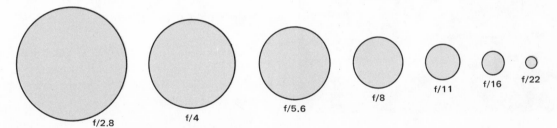

Fig. 7-4. Aperture (f-stop) is expressed as a fraction of the focal length of the lens. Focal length is the distance between the lens and the film when focus is set at infinity.

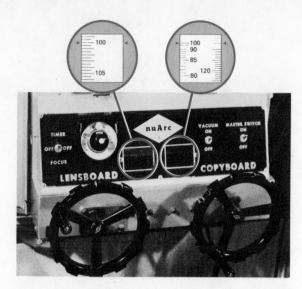

Fig. 7-5. Camera operator lines up percentage scales shown in inset by operating camera controls.

Fig. 7-6. Lights are fixed to camera frame and light up copy from an angle that will not cause glare on the film. Copyboard is in loading position.

Fig. 7-7. Timer measures in seconds and stops exposure when film has received enough light.

DARKROOM

A darkroom is light-tight so that the kind and amount of light can be controlled from inside the room. The access door must allow persons to enter and leave without disturbing the lighting conditions. Inside the darkroom, as shown in Fig. 7-8, should be space for processing and developing film. In addition,

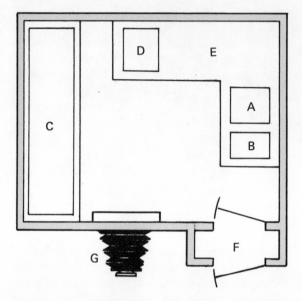

Fig. 7-8. Typical darkroom layout can be used for photography or graphic arts. A—Enlarger. B—Contact printer. C—Sink. D—Paper cutter. E—Storage. F—Light trap. G—Film case and bellows of process camera.

many school darkrooms include facilities for doing regular photography. Included are:

1. Plumbing and sink for developing and washing of film and photographic paper.
2. Electrical wiring for safelights and convenient outlets to run equipment.
3. Photographic equipment such as enlargers, process camera, contact printer, paper cutter and other equipment.
4. Storage for supplies and equipment.

DARKROOM SAFETY

The darkroom is used for all graphic arts film handling and processing. Care must be taken to avoid conditions which are unsafe. Certain safety precautions must be observed:

1. Do not try to mix chemicals under darkroom conditions. Use the main white light.

2. Wear rubber gloves and handle chemicals so as to avoid splashing into the eyes. Wash skin thoroughly if it has been in contact with chemicals.
3. Always pour acids into water; never pour water into acids. A violent reaction could occur.
4. Keep floors dry. Moisture can cause electrical shock or serious falls.
5. Store chemicals in safe containers where they can be easily reached. Plastic and stainless steel containers are safer; they will not shatter if dropped accidently.
6. All electrical items should be grounded. Never place electrical equipment near moisture. Never handle electrical equipment with wet hands or when any part of the body is in contact with water.

GRAPHIC ARTS FILM

Film used for graphic arts is made like the film used by photographers. It consists of several layers of material as shown in Fig. 7-9. The base, a transparent material of either acetate, plastic or polyester, is the thickest layer. It provides the strength to carry the other elements. Polyester films hold their size best and are always used in color work.

The antihalation coating prevents light rays from bouncing back into the light-sensitive layer where it could cause double images. This coating dissolves when the film is developed. The overcoating protects the emulsion from scratches during handling.

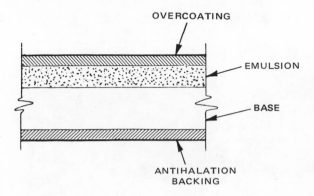

Fig. 7-9. Cross section of graphic arts film.

But the most important section is the emulsion or light-sensitive area. This coating contains the unexposed silver halides that are affected by the light. The exposed halides hold the latent (unseen) image until the film is developed. The silver halides change to metallic silver in the developer and turn black.

The emulsion on graphic arts (litho) film is called orthochromatic. It is sensitive to light rays other than red. Thus, the darkroom's red safelights do not affect or expose the film. Litho film emulsion is slow. It requires intense light and long exposure. It also has high contrast. The developed negative will have only dense black and clear areas.

PRODUCING LINE NEGATIVES

A line negative is the reverse image of line copy. It has only solid blacks and whites in it. Line copy can include ruled lines, spots, line drawings and type matter. The main tasks in producing the negative are:

1. Setting the exposure.
2. Mixing the chemicals.
3. Exposing the film.
4. Processing the film.

The steps for each of these tasks will be described in detail.

SETTING UP THE EXPOSURE

1. Place the camera-ready copy in the center of the camera's copyboard. Most copyboards have lines to make centering easier, Fig. 7-10.
2. Locate a gray scale in the margin, as shown in Fig. 7-10. It will indicate when development is complete.

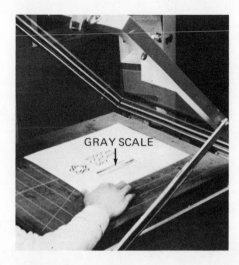

Fig. 7-10. Camera-ready copy is centered in copyboard.

3. Close the copyboard cover and rotate the board until it is upright.

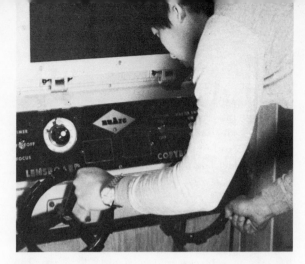

Fig. 7-11. Adjust the lens board and copyboard for percentage of enlargement or reduction.

Fig. 7-12. Check image on ground glass of film holder. It will be easier to see with darkroom lights off.

4. Set copyboard and lens board focusing scales to the percentages marked on the copy as in Fig. 7-11.
5. Set the f-stop according to instructions for the make of process camera. Otherwise, use the f/16 or f/22 scale. Adjust the aperture control for the percentage marked on the copy. See Fig. 7-3.
6. Check the image on the camera ground glass to see that it is centered and is sharp. See Fig. 7-12. This is easier in a darkened room.

MIXING CHEMICALS

1. Prepare the chemicals for processing film and place them in trays.
   a. Mix the litho type developer, either powder or liquid. Solution has two parts, A and B. Mix the powder following manufacturer's instructions. Liquid developer must be diluted. Use equal parts of A and B solution and place the new solution in the tray. Mixture will be discarded after use.
   b. In a second tray, place a stop bath. This is a diluted solution of acetic acid. It stops the developing process by neutralizing the developer.
   c. In a third tray, place a fixing bath or hypo. Mix powder or liquid according to manufacturer's instructions. This bath dissolves and washes away unexposed silver halides from the film base.
2. Turn on the water in the film washing area. Adjust temperature until approximately the same as the chemical baths. Fig. 7-13 shows a darkroom sink ready for developing.

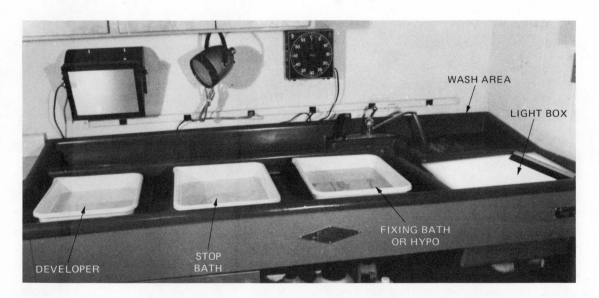

Fig. 7-13. Sink is set up for processing film before exposure is made.

EXPOSING FILM

The following procedures must be carried on under a red safelight:

1. Place a piece of film the correct size on the vacuum back of the process camera. Emulsion side must be toward the lens! Viewed under the red safelight, it is the light side, Fig. 7-14.
2. Center the film in the holder and close the camera back.
3. Set the timer for the lights and shutter. This must be determined by test in each graphic arts lab.
4. Press the "on" button and make the exposure.
5. When the lights go off and the shutter has closed, remove the film. It is now ready for the developer.

PROCESSING FILM

1. Lift the end of the developer tray and quickly slide film into the tray, Fig. 7-15. At the same

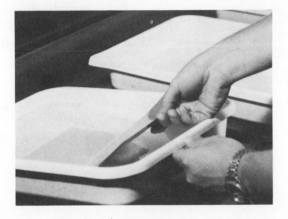

Fig. 7-14. Emulsion side of film looks lighter under safelight.

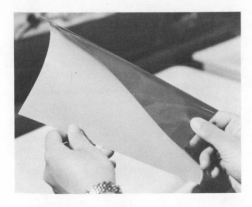

Fig. 7-15. Quickly slide film into tilted tray and lower the tray so solution washes over film quickly.

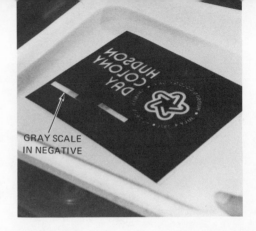

GRAY SCALE
IN NEGATIVE

Fig. 7-16. Development is complete when gray scales meet as shown.

time let the tray down easily and allow solution to wash over film in one wave-like motion. Rock tray slowly with an even motion until the two sections of the gray scale meet as in Fig. 7-16. This indicates that development is complete.
2. Transfer the film to the stop bath for about 10 seconds.
3. Transfer film to the fixing bath. Allow it to remain for twice the amount of time it takes for the film to clear.
4. Wash fixed film for at least 15 min. in running water.
5. As shown in Fig. 7-17, squeegee off excess water and hang film to dry, Fig. 7-18. A film dryer may be used if one is available.

NOTE: Maintain a clean darkroom. Do not splash chemicals. Avoid contamination of solutions by dipping unwashed hands from one to another in reverse order of developing. First wash solution from hands. Handle film only with dry hands.

PRODUCING HALFTONE NEGATIVES

Continuous tone copy such as photographs or artists' drawings, contain many gray tones between black and white. See photo on left in Fig. 7-19. It is

Fig. 7-17. Remove excess water with a squeegee.

Fig. 7-18. Film is hung to dry. Operator holds film carefully by edges to avoid damaging it.

not possible for a printing press to put less ink on one part of a printing plate so that it will print lighter tones. Something must be done to the plate before it is placed on the press. That "something" is the halftone process.

A screen is placed over the film when the process camera is photographing continuous tone copy. It breaks up the image into a series of dots. These dots are evenly spaced but vary in size. Look at Fig. 7-19. In light areas, the dot will be very small and in dark areas, very large. When the image is placed on the press, the dot areas print. Viewed from normal reading distance, the dots blend into tones of black and gray. The eye sees it like a photograph or a drawing. Fig. 7-19 shows a photo printed with a 120 line screen. The blowup magnifies the dot structure so you can see that it will print as a series of solid dots.

SCREEN MATERIALS

Most halftone screens used today are contact screens. The screen is actually a piece of film with a

Fig. 7-19. Boxed area is enlarged to show how halftone copy is broken up into dots for printing.

dot pattern in it. These screens come in magenta, an off-red color, or in a neutral tone of gray. The dot focus, as shown in Fig. 7-20, is less dense at the edges. The screen size refers to its fineness and is given in number of dots to the square inch. Commonly used sizes are 60, 65, 85, 120, 133 and 150. The smaller the number, the courser the screen. Newspapers use 65 line screens. Fine screens are used on coated paper stock.

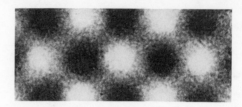

Fig. 7-20. Enlarged dot pattern shows that edges of dots are not sharply defined. This helps blend the dots together as the eye views the printed halftone.

Halftone screens should be handled carefully to avoid finger prints and scratches. Vacuum backed cameras must be used to hold screen and film in close contact. Screen and films are installed emulsion to emulsion.

AIDS FOR PRODUCING HALFTONES

Producing the halftone negative is different from producing the line negative. If not properly exposed, the negative will not make a good reproduction of the photograph. The camera operator must make two separate exposures. The first or main exposure is made for the benefit of the highlights and the middle tones in the photograph. The highlights are the white areas. The middle tones are the gray areas. The effect of this exposure is to assure that the dot pattern will hold detail in highlight areas. In the gray areas, the main exposure causes the middle tone dots to be medium in size.

The second or flash exposure places dots in the shadow areas of the halftone. Shadow areas are the black portions of the photograph. The proper balance of these two exposures is what produces a good halftone negative.

To produce a screened halftone negative, you will have to determine how much light various parts of the continuous tone copy is going to reflect. You will use several aids.

One of them will measure the ability of the copy to reflect. Another will calculate the proper settings for length of exposure and aperture opening.

One of the simplest and least costly aids is the KODAK EXPOSURE COMPUTER and the reflection density guide. The computer is calibrated to the equipment being used. It can be used along with the calibration gray scale, Fig. 7-21, to find the proper exposure.

Fig. 7-22. A reflection densitometer is an instrument used by commercial firms to measure reflective quality of photographs.

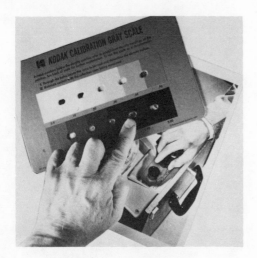

Fig. 7-21. Calibration gray scale being used to find shadow value of photograph.

Commercial plants will use a densitometer such as shown in Fig. 7-22. However, the simple aids described work very well and produce negatives of good quality.

COMPUTING THE HALFTONE EXPOSURE

The computer is calibrated by producing several test negatives until settings are found which produce the best negative. This procedure is explained in the instructions provided with the computer.

To produce a suitable negative, we shall assume that the computer is calibrated as in Fig. 7-23. An aperture of f/16 aligns with a 100 percent magnification. A density of .1 aligns with a 40 second exposure time. On the flash exposure table, a basic flash of 24 seconds is indicated. The screen range is 1.10.

Now proceed as follows:

1. Using the reflection density guide, evaluate the photograph.

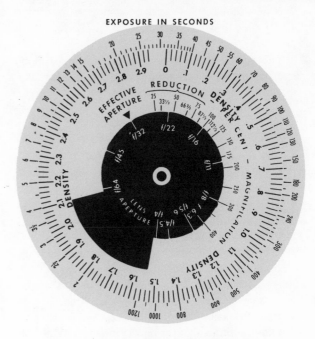

Fig. 7-23. Example of computer scale calibrated for a graphic arts process camera.

   a. Place the guide over the photograph and match the lightest area (highlight) with a square on the density guide as shown in Fig. 7-21. Note the number of the square.
   b. Find the darkest area (shadow) and match it to a dark square in the guide. Note the number of the square.
2. Supposing that the highlight was 0.00 and the shadow was 1.40, subtract the highlight from the shadow:

   1.40
   0.00

   1.40

   The answer is the density range of the photograph.
3. Now, suppose that the density of the screen being used is 1.10. This means that the screen can make a good halftone negative in one exposure of a

Basic Flash Exposure in Seconds*	Flash Exposure Times in Seconds for Excess Density Range								
	0	0.1	0.2	0.3	0.4	0.5	0.6	0.8	1.0
16	0	3½	6	8	9½	11	12	13½	14½
18	0	4	7	9	11	12	13½	15	16
20	0	4	7½	10	12	13½	15	17	18
22	0	4½	8½	11	13	15	16½	18½	20
24	0	5	9	12	14½	16	18	20	22
26	0	5½	10	13	15½	17½	19½	22	23½
28	0	6	10½	14	17	19	21	23½	25
30	0	6½	11	15	18	20½	22½	25	27
35	0	7	13	18	21	24	26	29	32
40	0	8	15	20	24	27	30	34	36
45	0	10	17	23	27	31	34	38	41
50	0	11	19	25	30	34	38	42	45
55	0	12	20	27	33	37	41	46	50
60	0	13	22	30	36	41	45	50	55
70	0	15	26	35	42	48	53	59	63
80	0	17	30	40	48	54	60	67	72

Fig. 7-24. Finding flash exposure time (color blocks) after excess density and basic exposure time is known.

photograph having a density range of 1.10. Subtract the density range of the screen from the density range of the photograph:

1.40
1.10
.30

The result is an excess density of .30. An additional exposure will be needed to make a good negative.

4. Find the additional exposure time by locating the excess density column and the basic flash exposure time on the FLASH EXPOSURE TABLE, Fig. 7-24. The flash exposure will be made with an auxiliary lamp that hangs over the vacuum back of the camera, Fig. 7-25. The light source is a low-wattage bulb behind an OA (yellow) filter.

5. Find the main exposure time. Refer to the computer and note that the highlight density 0.00 (the highlight density of the photograph) aligns with 32 seconds. This is the main exposure time. No additional calculations are needed for magnification or reduction. They are taken care of by the modifications on the camera focus scale. This is explained in the section on exposing the line negative.

MAKING THE EXPOSURES

1. Prepare chemical baths as described in the section on line negatives.
2. Place litho type film on the camera back, emulsion up.
3. Place contact screen on top of the film emulsion down.
4. Turn on the vacuum, close the film back and make the main exposure for 32 seconds.
5. Open the camera back. Leave the vacuum on and the screen in place.
6. Make the flash exposure for 12 seconds.

Fig. 7-25. Camera back is open for flash exposure using yellow light at ceiling.

7. Turn off the vacuum. Remove the contact screen. Place it carefully in its protective envelope.
8. Develop the film as described in developing the line negative. Set the timer for 2 1/2 min. After 2 min. of constant agitation, allow the tray to remain still for remainder of development time.
9. Move film through the baths as described in developing line film.
10. After film is dry, inspect the dots. Fig. 7-26 shows the general dot patterns for the various percentages. The camera operator tries to get a 10 percent dot pattern in the highlight areas of the negative and a 90 percent dot in the shadow

areas of the negative. Note: The negative, being a reverse of the photograph, shows highlight areas as dark, while shadow area is light or clear.

As the camera operator gains experience, a gray scale will be placed in the copy margin so that he or she can evaluate the developing negative by checking the dots in the scale. Developing time is added or subtracted after the inspection to get the halftone quality desired.

SPECIAL TECHNIQUES

A photograph with little difference between highlight and shadow is said to be flat. Its appearance can be improved by a bump exposure. This is a short exposure made without the contact screen. The length of the exposure is about 10 percent of the main exposure which is reduced by about the same amount. Vacuum must remain on during the several exposures so that the film does not move. Developing follows the regular procedure. Fig. 7-27 shows the results of a bump exposure.

MAKING CONTACT NEGATIVES

Duplicate negatives, contact proofs and reverses are made by essentially the same process as the contact print. Two special pieces of equipment, a vacuum frame and a contact printing lamp, are required, Fig. 7-28.

The contact proof is like a contact photograph except that the negative, in this case, is screened. It shows how the illustration will look when it is printed. The print is made on photostabilization paper.

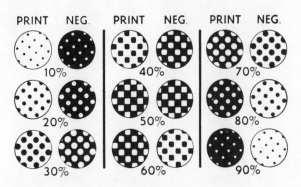

Fig. 7-26. Enlargment shows general dot pattern of the negative and how it will print at different percentages.

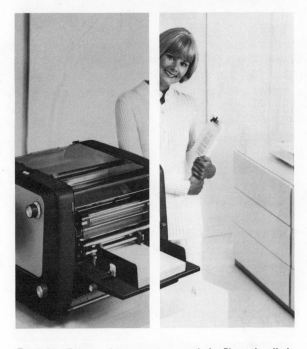

Fig. 7-27. Effects of bump exposure. Left. Photo has little contrast between highlights and shadow areas. Right. Bump exposure has given the same photo more snap and contrast.

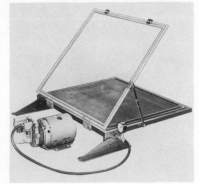

Fig. 7-28. Contact printing setup for making duplicate negatives, proofs, and reverses. Left. Making the exposure. Center. Contact printing lamp and controls. Right. Vacuum frame with pump. (nuArc Co., Inc.)

Fig. 7-29. Example of a reversal. Left. Film positive used to produce a negative print. Right. Negative print has image area in white.

In a reversal, the image area — such as type or illustrations — appears as white and the background as black. Making it requires an extra step in photoconversion. A film positive must be made from the film negative. The camera operator will place a sheet of film emulsion side up on the contact frame. The film negative is placed on top (also emulsion side up) and an exposure is made. After developing the film, positive looks like the film at left in Fig. 7-29. The final step is to make a print from the film positive. Positives are used in screen process printing to make the photographic stencils.

DUOTONES

A DUOTONE is a halftone printed in two colors. Two halftones are made from the same photograph. The procedure for making the negative film is the same except that the screen angle is changed for one. The darkest color halftone negative is made with the screen placed square in the copyboard. This produces a screen angle of 45 deg. The screen in the second negative is rotated 30 deg. See Fig. 7-30.

Fig. 7-31. Posterizing makes a photograph look like a brush drawing done in black and one or two colors. Highlights, middletones and shadows are produced in separate negatives.

POSTERIZATION

POSTERIZATION is exposing continuous tone copy as though it were line copy. No screen is placed in the process camera while the film is exposed. Underexposing and overexposing give very different results.

A two-color posterized print is made by underexposing the color negative (printer) while overexposing the black negative (printer), Fig. 7-31.

Fig. 7-30. Duotone is printed from two halftone negatives. Left. Negative for black is generally overexposed to reduce dots from highlights. Extra flash exposure emphasizes shadow areas. Center. Negative for color is given reduced exposure, but no flash exposure. Right. Completed duotone.

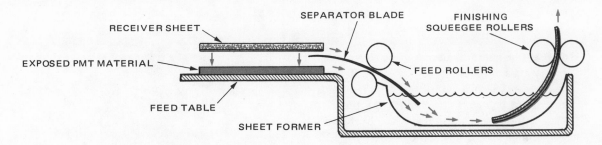

Fig. 7-32. Exposed negative and receiver sheet are fed into PMT processor.

PHOTOMECHANICAL TRANSFER (PMT)

The PMT process is a method of quickly producing enlargements, reductions or same size artwork for camera-ready copy. It saves the original art.

A PMT negative film is exposed with a reproduction camera and then is fed into a processor along with a receiver sheet as shown in Fig. 7-32. The film and receiver sheet come out of the processor stuck together, Fig. 7-33. In 30 seconds the sheets are separated. The black and white image is fixed to the receiver sheet.

FOUR COLOR PROCESS

Producing photographs in full color is called process color printing. The camera work required to separate the color of the original full color photograph into suitable screen negatives is difficult. Certainly, it is beyond the level of work expected in a basic graphic arts course. Yet, it is possible to understand the basic principles that make the process work.

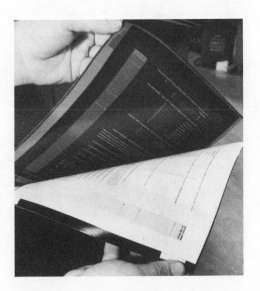

Fig. 7-33. Receiver sheet is peeled from PMT negative. Image has been transferred to the receiver as a positive.

All process color printing is made up of three primary colors and black. You can think of the colors as ink also. The primary colors are:

1. Magenta (red).
2. Cyan (blue).
3. Yellow.

When printed together cyan, magenta and yellow can reproduce all of the colors you see in a color illustration or photograph. However, black is almost always added to improve the general appearance of the illustration.

But first the cyan, magenta and yellow must be separated out of the color copy or photograph. Four screened negatives — also called printers — are made using a process camera. As each negative is exposed, the light is made to shine through a different filter.

1. A red filter makes the negative for cyan.
2. A green filter makes the negative for magenta.
3. A blue filter makes the negative for yellow.
4. No filter is needed to make the black negative. Or, the black negative may be exposed through all three filters.

To see more clearly how a color negative is made, consider what happens when a negative is exposed through a red filter:

1. The filter lets through all of the red in the color photograph but very little of the green and blue.
2. When the negative is developed, it becomes very dense in the areas where there is red. The areas where the photo has cyan will be thin enough for light to burn through.
3. The negative is used to burn a plate for the printing press. But the light cannot shine through the dense area representing the red portions of the photograph. However, it does shine through the thin areas where the photograph is cyan (blue and green).
4. Therefore, when the plate is processed, the dot pattern will be heavy in the area representing cyan.

There will be no dot pattern in the area representing magenta and yellow.

5. The dot area will pick up ink and print the ink on the sheet of paper coming through the press. Of course, cyan ink is used so that it will be the same color as those parts of the photograph.

The same process is used for producing the negatives and plates for magenta and yellow. Black, as explained, is produced without a filter or by using all the filters.

Modern equipment reduces the hard work of making color separations. A scanner, see Fig. 7-34, is used by large printing plants.

GRAVURE PHOTOGRAPHY

Gravure printing requires a totally different camera technique. The photographs are reproduced on continuous tone film similar to the type used in regular photography. Special handling of the material is then necessary in the making of the image carrier.

SPECIAL EFFECTS SCREENS

Sometimes, screens in special patterns are used to produce halftones, Fig. 7-35. The processing of halftone material using such screens is exactly the same as with regular contact screens.

QUIZ – UNIT 7

1. When film is exposed to camera-ready copy, in preparation for making an image carrier, the process is called _____.

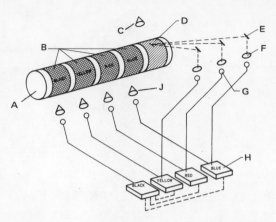

Fig. 7-34. Schematic of scanner which makes automatic color separations. A—Rotating drum. B—Negatives. C—Lamp. D—Color transparency. E—Mirrors. F—Filters. G—Photoelectric cells. H—Color computers. J—Glow lamps. Photoelectric cells pick up reflected color and sends impulses to computers. Computers act on the impulses, expose negatives by controlling light through glow lamps.
(Printing Developments, Inc.)

2. List the kinds of process cameras used in exposing graphic arts film.
3. Which of the following are part of the process camera:
   a. Contact film.   e. Lens board.
   b. Copyboard.   f. Light source.
   c. Darkroom.   g. Safety light.
   d. Film holder.   h. Timer.
4. A darkroom has different kinds of safelights but all light can be kept out if necessary. True or False?
5. _____ film is not sensitive to red light.
6. A _____ negative reproduces only solid black and white and a _____ negative reproduces shades of black and white using a dot pattern.
7. Density of a photograph is checked with a _____ _____ _____ or a _____.
8. Name the three colors of filters used in making a color separation.

Fig. 7-35. Special effects in two halftones at right were produced by special contact screens.

IMAGE CARRIERS

1. How image carriers differ for various printing processes.
2. Making photo-offset lithographic plates.
3. Preparing letterpress forms for the press.
4. Making a silk-screen stencil.
5. Preparing an intaglio engraving.

An IMAGE CARRIER is any kind of material on which an image can be placed for printing purposes. It will receive ink and then transfer the ink onto paper or other printing material. Image carriers are made of:

1. Metal.
2. Paper.
3. Plastic.
4. Rubber and other materials.

This unit will discuss image carriers used for photo-offset lithography, letterpress, silk screen and intaglio printing. Basic differences in these image carriers are shown in Fig. 8-1.

In the letterpress process, type generated on metal often becomes the image carrier. But even in letterpress operations, large commercial shops do not print from the original type. They make printing plates. Each process has a way of producing printing plates.

MAKING OFFSET LITHOGRAPHIC PLATES

Making an image carrier for an offset press usually involves shining light through a negative onto a light-sensitive sheet of metal. After processing, the plate is placed on the press. There are two parts to the process:

1. Stripping. This procedure attaches the negative onto a heavy yellow paper sheet called a "goldenrod." Windows are cut in the goldenrod to expose the image area to the light during the "burning" operation. Burning is another word used for exposing the plate to light.
2. Platemaking. In this procedure, the image on the

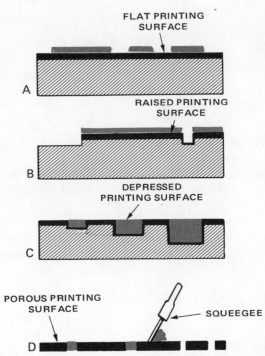

Fig. 8-1. Image carrier surfaces for different printing processes. A—Lithography. Ink clings only to the greasy image area of a flat surface. B—Letterpress. Image is on raised portion of surface. C—Intaglio. Image is in the depressed portion of the surface. D—Silk screen. Image area is porous. Ink is squeezed through tiny holes to material being printed.

negative is transferred onto the plate which will be placed on the press.

THE GOLDENROD

The goldenrod has markings which speed up the stripping operations by showing where to position copy. Fig. 8-2 identifies the following:

1. Pin registration holes. These are used when multiple exposures (burns) are made on a plate.

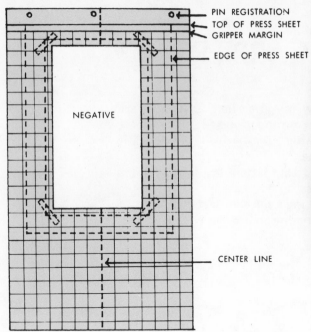

Fig. 8-2. Goldenrod holds negative and is often marked with lines to help in positioning the negative film on it.

2. Top of press sheet line, which shows where the top of the press sheet will fall.
3. Gripper margin. An indication of where grippers on the press hold the sheet as it goes through the press. (If type or illustrations are placed in this area they will not print.)
4. Centerline and edge of sheet lines to help in centering film and locating the edge of the press sheet.

STRIPPING PROCEDURE

Stripping is a simple task if these steps are followed:

1. Square up a goldenrod on the light table, as shown in Fig. 8-3, and tape it down.

Fig. 8-3. T-square and triangles used to square up goldenrod on light table.

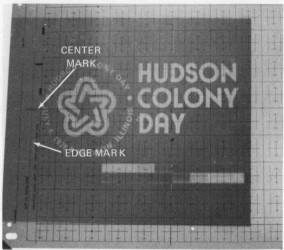

Fig. 8-4. Center negative beneath the goldenrod.

2. With emulsion side down, slide the negative under the goldenrod. (If you can read the negative, the emulsion is down.)
3. Carefully position the negative under the goldenrod, Fig. 8-4.
4. Cut two small windows in the goldenrod and place tape across them. This will temporarily hold negative and goldenrod together, Fig. 8-5.
5. Loosen taped corners and turn the flat over.
6. Tape negative to goldenrod, Fig. 8-6.
7. Turn the flat over again and cut away the goldenrod in the image area so the light can pass through during exposure. See Fig. 8-7.

STRIPPING HALFTONES

Halftones, if any, are stripped in as follows:

1. Flop the flat so the negative reads wrong, Fig. 8-8. Place the halftone negatives in the windows left for them, emulsion side up. They must fill the

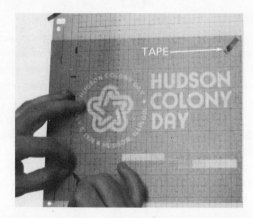

Fig. 8-5. Tape is placed across small hole cut in goldenrod to hold negative in position.

Fig. 8-6. Corners and edges of film must be taped to goldenrod.

Fig. 8-7. Window is cut in the goldenrod with a knife to expose the image area.

Fig. 8-8. Halftones are stripped into "windows" left in the line negative.

window area without covering any type.

2. Fasten the halftones to the flat with small pieces of tape at the corners as in Fig. 8-9.

OPAQUING

The completely assembled flat must be inspected for pinholes. These are small clear areas that will print as unwanted black spots. They must be painted with OPAQUE, a light-retarding paint. When thinned with a small amount of water, the opaque is easily applied with a small camel hair brush, Fig. 8-10.

When opaquing is completed, the flat is ready for the platemaking operation. Sometimes, holes need to be punched for double burning or two-color printing. See Fig. 8-11.

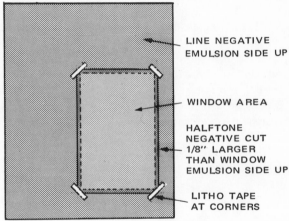

LINE NEGATIVE EMULSION SIDE UP

WINDOW AREA

HALFTONE NEGATIVE CUT 1/8" LARGER THAN WINDOW EMULSION SIDE UP

LITHO TAPE AT CORNERS

Fig. 8-9. Instructions for stripping in halftones.

Fig. 8-10. Pinholes in the negative are coated with a water base liquid that blocks out light.

Fig. 8-11. Hand punch is used to make holes in the flat if they are needed for double burning or multicolor register.

EXPOSING THE OFFSET PLATE

The image on the flat is transferred to a press plate by a contact printing process. It is a good deal like making contact prints in photography. However, a few additional steps are included.

Offset printing plates are of many different types. All are made up of a thin sheet or base on which is placed a light-sensitive material. When this surface is exposed to a strong light, a chemical change takes place. Thus, when the surface is treated with the developers and properly rubbed up, the image will become an ink-receptive surface.

Fig. 8-12. Locate plate and flat in the platemaker. (nuArc Co., Inc.)

The plates used by most schools are presensitized. They are available in paper, plastic, paper-backed metal foil and metal. Each is suited to a particular use. Some are meant to be exposed under a negative while others are burned under a positive.

Follow these steps to burn (expose) a plate:

1. Turn off the room lights and turn on a yellow safelight.
2. Remove a plate from the supply and punch holes, if needed, for double burning or color work.
3. Lay the flat on top of the plate and position both in the plate burner, Fig. 8-12. CAUTION: If register pins are needed, use short ones to avoid cracking the glass when the cover is lowered.
4. Close the cover and turn on the vacuum pump so the flat and the plate are pressed tightly together.
5. If a flip-top platemaker is used, turn it over so flat is facing down, Fig. 8-13.

Fig. 8-13. Flip-top platemaker shown here has its light source inside cabinet. Other types have light source above.

6. Set timer and make the exposure.
7. Return flip-top to original loading position. Turn off the vacuum.

PLATE PROCESSING

Plates are given a chemical treatment to bring out the image. This treatment varies with the type of plate used. The following procedure is used with additive plates of the type made by 3M Company:

1. Place the plate in a sink or on a good flat surface.
2. Pour process gum over the plate and, working with a sponge in a circular motion, spread the gum over the entire surface as in Fig. 8-14. The process gum removes unexposed coating in the non-image areas.
3. Pour on a small amount of plate developer. With another sponge, spread it over the plate with the

Fig. 8-14. Process gum is carefully spread over entire plate surface.

Fig. 8-15. Plate developer is added to surface. If properly exposed, a red image will appear.

same circular motion used in the previous step. See Fig. 8-15.

4. Go over the plate with the gum sponge and then wipe it dry with a clean wipe. The plate is now ready for the press.

RELIEF IMAGE CARRIERS

Many times the type set by hand or by machine is placed directly on the press and becomes the image carrier. Special preparation must be made to secure the type in a frame where it cannot move around during printing. This frame, called a CHASE, is made of iron. Its purpose is to form a support so the type can be squeezed from all four sides.

LOCKING UP A TYPEFORM

Securing the type in the form is called lockup. The typeform, if small, is slid off the galley onto the stone or imposing table. Next, the printer will place the chase around the type and fill the empty space on all sides with furniture, Fig. 8-16.

Furniture is made in various lengths and widths. Included are the reglets. These are thin wood strips 6 and 12 points thick. From a distance they look like lead and slugs. Furniture is stored in furniture racks according to size: 2, 3, 4, 5, 6, 8 and 10 picas wide and from 10 picas to 60 picas long. See Fig. 8-17.

When the chase is being locked up for a hand-fed platen press, place the form so the sheet of printing paper can be fed at or near the center of the press. The head (top) of the form should be located at either the left or the bottom of the chase as you face

Fig. 8-16. Furniture (blocking of wood and metal) is placed around the typeform.

Fig. 8-17. Storage rack keeps wood furniture sorted according to size and length. (Hamilton Mfg. Co.)

it on the stone. The longer side of the chase should face you as you work. The shape of the printing paper determines where the head of the form will be placed. For easier feeding, the long way of the sheet should be parallel with the long way of the chase.

When the form is properly located in the chase, place furniture around it. Two styles of lockup are shown in Fig. 8-18. The top photograph shows the CHASER method. Each of the four pieces of furniture next to the typeform is longer than the form. As pressure is applied by tightening the quoins, the furniture slides past ends of furniture running at right angles. The bottom photograph, Fig. 8-18, shows the SQUARED method of lockup. Most printers prefer the chaser method.

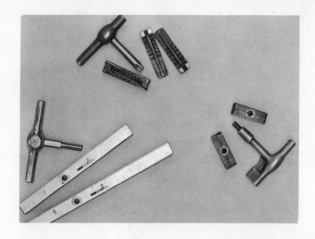

Fig. 8-19. Quoins are adjustable blocks which can expand or contract by adjusting them with the T-shaped tools called keys.

the form. Reglets are placed on both sides of the quoins to protect the quoins. Three styles of quoins, and quoin keys are shown in Fig. 8-19.

When furniture and quoins are in place, tighten the quoins just enough to square the type. Place a planer block on top of the type. Tap the block lightly with a mallet, Fig. 8-20. This is done to make sure the type is squarely on its feet or aligned. Tighten the quoins. Place the quoin key under one corner of the chase.

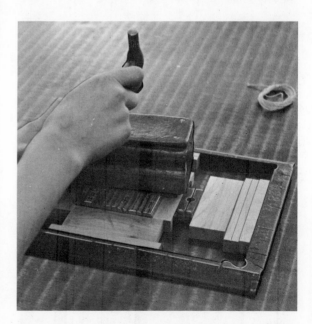

Fig. 8-20. Planer block is tapped to align type for proper height. The pressure forces each line downward to rest on top of the stone.

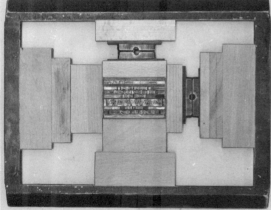

Fig. 8-18. Locked up forms. Top. Chaser type lockup. Bottom. Squared type lockup.

Place quoins at the top and the right side of the form to hold the type in the chase. The quoins should be located near the typeform, but there should always be a piece of furniture between the quoin and

Press gently on the type with your fingers to see if the type will stay firmly in the chase, Fig. 8-21. Should any lines of type push down, your type

Fig. 8-21. One side of chase is raised to see if type is firmly locked in.

justification is incorrect. It should be corrected so the type will lock securely in the chase. This is called "checking the form for lift."

When the form is properly justified, it is ready for the press. This procedure is discussed in the next unit.

PLATES FOR LETTERPRESS

Plates for letterpress are of two major types:

1. Primary.
2. Secondary.

Primary plates consist of line etchings and halftones. The photographic and preparatory operations are similar to those performed for offset plates. The major difference is that the plates are made wrong reading. Letterpress prints directly from the plate. No blanket cylinder reverses the image as in offset.

LINE ENGRAVINGS

A line engraving or etching is a plate that reproduces line work. This is copy which is black and white with no intermediate shades. Fig. 8-22 shows a line engraving as it is made up for the form. It is locked up in the chase with the type for printing.

The engraving is made by placing the line negative on a piece of presensitized photoengravers' metal and exposing it to produce a reverse image. The metal plate is etched in an etching machine to obtain a relief (raised) image. (Etching is a chemical process which wears away some of the metal.) The relief plate is mounted on a block the same height as type.

HALFTONE ENGRAVINGS

The halftone engraving allows us to print pictures in the letterpress printing process. The procedures are the same as for making the halftone negative for offset. As with the line etching above, the halftone for letterpress must be made in reverse so that it can print directly from the plate. Fig. 8-23 shows a halftone engraving. It also is mounted on a block type-high so that it can be locked up in the chase.

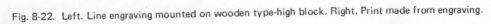

Fig. 8-22. Left. Line engraving mounted on wooden type-high block. Right. Print made from engraving.

Fig. 8-23. Halftones for relief printing are mounted type-high on wooden bases.

COMBINATION PLATES

Because of improved camera techniques and photographic equipment, commercial printers are using complete plates rather than type and plate lockups. Type and illustrations are prepared for photography, as in the offset process. A full plate is made including halftones, line etchings and type. The plate is mounted type-high if it is to be printed on a cylinder or platen press. If the job is to be printed on a rotary press, the plate is used as a master and duplicate plates are made for the press.

PLASTIC LETTERPRESS PLATES

The letterpress industry also used plastic (synthetic) materials for printing plates. This plate, made photographically, can be mounted type-high for flat printing or it can be curved and attached to a high-speed rotary press.

DUPLICATE PLATES

Many letterpress shops do not print with the original engravings, but use them only as masters for making duplicates. Using duplicates for printing protects the more expensive originals from being

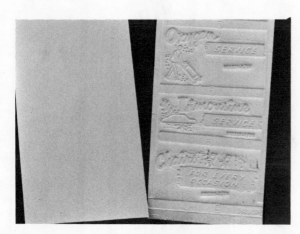

Fig. 8-24. Stereotype material. Left. Mat stock. Right. Mat has received impression of type and illustrations.

damaged on the press. This is particularly true in color printing. Type, as well as engravings, is plated. The duplicate plates may be plastic or rubber, stereotypes or electrotypes.

MAKING STEREOTYPES

To make a stereotype, the original engraving and the type are locked up as for printing. A special papier-mache (mat paper) is laid over the form and placed in a molding press. Under heavy pressure, the softer mat paper is molded around the type characters and illustrations. The result is a mold called a matrix or mat. Fig. 8-24 shows stereotype matrix material before and after it is formed in the molding press.

The matrix is placed in a casting box while molten type metal is poured into the caster. A stereotype plate is formed as the molten material flows over the mat. Fig. 8-25 shows a curved cast stereotype. This type of printing plate is used in newspaper work.

MAKING ELECTROTYPES

An electrotype is a precision printing plate used for color printing and for more exacting work than a stereotype.

Fig. 8-25. Plates can be cast to fit around cylinder of rotary presses. (Greeley Colorado Tribune)

As in stereotyping, the first step in making an electrotype, is to make a matrix in a special hydraulic press. The matrix material, sheet lead, plastic or a wax, is capable of more precise reproductions.

The matrix, after being formed, is made electrically conductive by spraying it with silver, or coating it with graphite. It is then placed in a special tank, where electroplating forms a shell on the matrix. The shell becomes the printing face of the new plate. Type metal is used to back up this thin shell and the electrotype is either made type-high by mounting on a block or is prepared for use on a rotary press, Fig. 8-26.

SCREEN PROCESS IMAGE CARRIERS

Image carriers for the screen process are called stencils. Ink or screen process paint is forced through the openings of the stencil, then through the screen, leaving a design on the printing material.

A stencil or image carrier is prepared in either of two ways:

1. By hand cutting.
2. By photography.

HAND-CUT STENCILS

Hand-cut stencil material is made up of a thin film of gelatin on either a wax paper or mylar base. This material is transparent and allows the design to show through for cutting.

Stencil film may be either lacquer base or water base. One type uses lacquer thinner and the other type uses water to adhere the stencil to the screen. This procedure is discussed in the next unit.

HAND CUTTING THE STENCIL

To produce a hand-cut stencil:

1. Cut a piece of stencil film from the supply roll.
2. Cut the film to allow a 2 in. margin all around the design.
3. Attach the design to the back of the stencil with tape.
4. With a sharp knife, cut out the design, tracing with the knife along the lines of the original. See Fig. 8-27. Cutting should be done on a hard, smooth surface. Hardboard or glass is suggested. Use light pressure on the knife. Cut only through the gelatinous layer. Do not cut or emboss the backing sheet. (Embossing is a ridge raised on the underside of the backing sheet by pressing down too hard on the knife.)
5. Strip away the gelatin layer (film) in the image area. Fig. 8-28 shows a stencil with the gelatin

Fig. 8-26. Left. Wood-mounted electrotype is used on flat bed press. Right. Curved electro fits on drum of rotary press.

Fig. 8-27. Sharp knife is used to cut design into gelatinous layer of stencil. Design shows clearly through the stencil.

Fig. 8-28. Stencil at upper right is ready for printing. Printer is marking guidelines for positioning film on silk screen.

Fig. 8-29. Material for preparing a photographic stencil. Upper right. Camera-ready copy. Lower right. Film negative. Lower center. Film positive. Lower left. Chemicals for developing film.

Fig. 8-30. The light-sensitive stencil and film positive are placed in the platemaker to make an exposure.

film stripped away. The stencil is ready to be used, or it can be stored until needed.

PHOTOGRAPHIC STENCILS

Photographic stencil material looks the same as the hand-cut material. The film coating has been mixed with chemicals that are light-sensitive. When light strikes the light-sensitive mixture, the mixture hardens. Being light-sensitive, it must be handled in subdued light. Yellow light is considered safe.

To make the photographic stencil you will need a transparent film positive of the image you want to reproduce. See Fig. 8-29. The photographic film can be purchased in cut sheets or in a large roll. Each manufacturer has the correct chemicals or developer to bring out the image.

MAKING THE PHOTOGRAPHIC STENCIL

1. Cut the stencil material about 2 in. larger than the image area.
2. Lay the film positive over the stencil material as shown in Fig. 8-30.
3. Place this sandwich into a platemaker as in making offset plates.
4. Turn on the vacuum to hold the positive and the film material in close contact.
5. Flip the vacuum holder over to direct the film toward the light source.
6. Turn on the light for about 90 seconds. Exposure times may vary due to equipment differences. Test for the best exposure.
7. Place the exposed film in the developing solutions for 90 seconds at 100 deg. F (38 C).
8. Immediately after development, place the stencil

on a piece of glass in the developing sink and spray it carefully with 100 deg. F (38 C) water, Fig. 8-31.

9. When the design has washed out, change the temperature of the water spray to 75 deg. F (24 C) to harden the stencil.
10. Place the stencil in the screen process frame while it is still wet. The adhering procedure is discussed in Unit 9.

Fig. 8-31. Careful washing with warm water removes gelatin from image area of stencil.

INTAGLIO IMAGE CARRIERS

Intaglio or gravure image carriers are large copper-coated cylinders. Fig. 8-32 shows copper plating of a press cylinder. After plating, the cylinder is polished to provide a smooth printing surface. Negatives and positives are prepared in a camera room.

The copper cylinder itself is not sensitive. Instead, a special material known as carbon tissue is sensitized.

Fig. 8-32. Copper plating cylinder of rotogravure press. (Denver Post)

Fig. 8-34. Backing paper is being removed from surface of carbon tissue.

Fig. 8-33. Carbon tissue is placed on copper-plated rotogravure cylinder.

Fig. 8-35. Etching designs into rotogravure cylinder.

The image and screen pattern are exposed to this carbon tissue material.

The screen pattern is exposed to the tissue first, then a continuous tone positive is exposed to the same material. This makes the dot pattern in gravure work different than the dot pattern used in letterpress and lithography. In gravure printing, everything is screened, even type matter.

The carbon tissue is put on the copper-plated cylinder in a LAYDOWN machine, Fig. 8-33. This device allows the carbon tissue to be put in register so the pages will print correctly. If color is used, it will print in the correct position.

After the carbon tissue has been put in place, the backing paper is removed, leaving just the gelatin surface with the image on the cylinder. This is called developing. See Fig. 8-34. The gelatin becomes an acid-resist material.

The cylinder is put into an etching bath, which eats away metal to produce wells in the copper. Fig. 8-35 shows this operation. The light areas of the picture allow only a shallow etch; the dark areas allow a deeper etch. Handwork, called staging, is frequently necessary to complete the plate.

Rotofilm is being used in some shops in place of carbon tissue. The processes are the same, but the Rotofilm appears as a visible image before being transferred to the cylinder. This helps in quality control.

QUIZ – UNIT 8

1. Describe the two parts of the process of making a lithographic image carrier.
2. During exposure of a light-sensitive offset plate, the light shines through the transparent paper which is called the goldenrod. True or False?
3. Offset plates are give a _____ _____ to bring out the image.
4. A _____ is the frame which holds the letterpress form in the printing press.
5. Describe a stereotype and explain how it is made.
6. The stencil used in silk-screen process is made up of a _____ sheet of _____ _____ or _____ and a thin layer of _____ material.
7. Name the two types of stencils used in silk-screening.

IMAGE TRANSFER AND PRESSWORK

1. Placing the image carrier on the press.
2. Press preparation and operation in offset lithography.
3. Relief printing on the platen press.
4. Screen process presswork using either hand-cut or photo stencils.
5. Printing by the intaglio method.

All printing processes have a system that brings ink and substrate (any material to be printed) into contact with the image carrier. The system works more or less automatically so that a large number of copies may be printed in a short time.

In every printing method this system sees to it that only the image on the carrier receives the printing ink. Image transfer mechanisms are designed to bring carrier, ink and substrate together. The mechanism used is a PRINTING PRESS. The job of the press is:

1. Apply the ink to the image area of the carrier.
2. Press the substrate against the inked image carrier.
3. Move the printed matter away so the steps can be repeated over and over again.

THE LITHOGRAPHIC (OFFSET) PRESS

Offset presses, Fig. 9-1, print from a flat image carrier. The image area accepts ink because the surface is greasy. The non-image area is receptive to water and the wet surfaces will not hold ink. Offset presses, Fig. 9-2, combine six systems.

1. Feeder system. It has guides which hold the stock and suction fingers which pick up one sheet at a time, delivering it to the rollers and webs in the register system.
2. Register system. Rollers and webs or tapes move the sheet up to the cylinders which make up the transfer system. Side guides, called JOGGERS, line up the sheet so it will enter the image transfer

Fig. 9-1. Small or large, every lithographic offset press has six basic systems. This unit is inexpensive and easy to operate. (Addressograph-Multigraph Corp.)

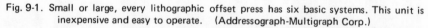

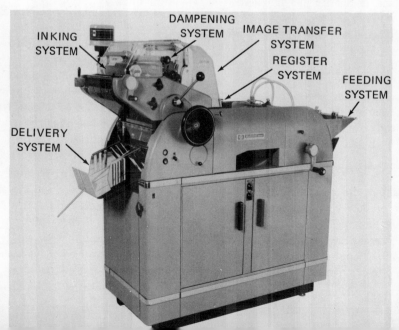

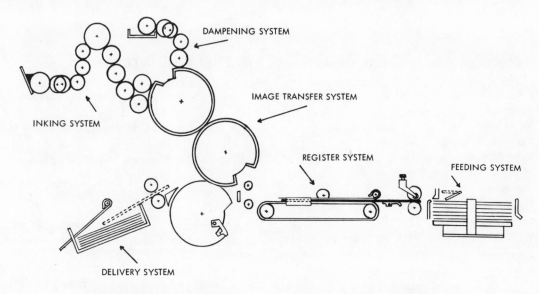

Fig. 9-2. Printing press systems are designed to work as one continuous unit.

system properly lined up. A stop will halt the forward motion of the sheet in the exact spot for it to be picked up by the cylinder.

3. Image transfer system. It holds the image carrier and presses the sheet of stock against the inked impression.

4. Dampening system. Water is held in a well and distributed evenly over the non-image area of the plate by a series of rollers. If not dampened, the non-image areas would pick up some ink.

5. Inking system. Ink is carried by rollers from an ink

well and spread over the image area of the plate.

6. Delivery system. This system takes the sheets from the printing unit and stacks them into a pile on a rack or skid.

A small table top offset press is shown in Fig. 9-3.

PRESS SAFETY

To avoid injury while operating presses observe the following safety rules:

Fig. 9-3. Inexpensive duplicator uses offset process. (A.B. Dick Co.)

1. Never operate equipment without the approval of your instructor.
2. Follow the recommended procedures for press operation.
3. Never wear loose clothing around presses.
4. Tie back long hair.
5. Keep isles and areas around the press clear.
6. Remove litter, grease and oil from floors and platforms.
7. Handle paper carefully to avoid muscle strain, sprains and cuts.
8. Do not oil presses while they are in motion; never reach over or into a press while it is running.
9. Make sure that all guards are in place before operating the press.
10. Use only approved solvents; store them in safety containers.
11. Dispose of solvent soaked cleaning rags in safe containers.
12. Do not leave tools where they will fall into the press or where someonce can trip over them.

MAKE-READY AND OPERATION

Your introduction to the offset printing press may be on a press such as the one illustrated in Fig. 9-1 or the duplicator shown in Fig. 9-3.

These are inexpensive presses. Although they are limited to small sheet sizes, they are well suited to teaching basic offset presswork.

The following procedures explain the proper method for operating the A.B. Dick model 310. Operation of other offset lithographic presses will be similar. Refer to the manufacturer's directions.

Fig. 9-4. Feeder guide is adjusted for size of paper.

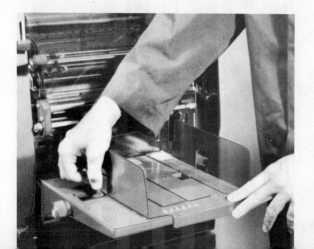

GATHERING MATERIALS

Gather materials needed for offset presswork:

1. Image carrier (plate). Preparation of the carrier is explained in Unit 8.
2. Paper stock of proper size. Cutting procedures are explained in Unit 10.
3. Ink, clean-up liquid and clean rags.

The fountain solution is mixed with water following the manufacturer's instructions. Use offset or lithographic ink.

SETTING UP THE OFFSET PRESS

1. Set the feeder system to fit the paper size, Fig. 9-4. The register system, in this case, is a part of the feeder system.
2. Fan the sheets. Place them in the feeder, Fig. 9-5.

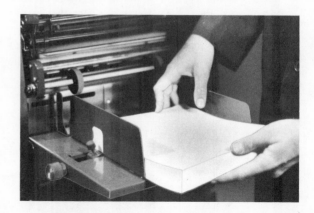

Fig. 9-5. Paper stock is carefully placed in the feeder.

3. Run one sheet through the press without turning on the ink and dampening systems, so that you can set the delivery system, Fig. 9-6.
4. Run several more sheets through the press to

Fig. 9-6. As sheet comes through press, operator aligns side guide of receiving tray with edge of sheet.

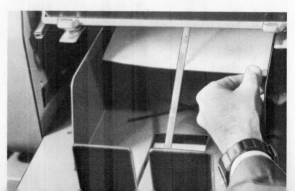

make sure feeder and delivery systems are working.

5. On presses with an integrated dampening system, the press must be inked up before fountain solution is placed in the water fountain. Be sure to follow instructions in the manufacturer's handbook for whatever press is used.

6. When the ink is well distributed on the rollers, the dampening solution can be poured into the water fountain.

7. Attach the head of the image carrier (plate), Fig. 9-7, to the plate cylinder.

Fig. 9-9. Left. Press sheet is compared with the camera-ready copy. Image is too low on the sheet. Press register needs to be adjusted.

Fig. 9-7. Head of image carrier (plate) is being attached to the plate cylinder.

8. Attach the tail of the image carrier to the cylinder, Fig. 9-8.

9. Print several copies of the job and check the quality against the layout as shown in Fig. 9-9. Check also that the image is printing in the proper position on the sheet.

10. Reset the head adjustment, Fig. 9-10, if image is too low on the sheet. Reset side guides on the

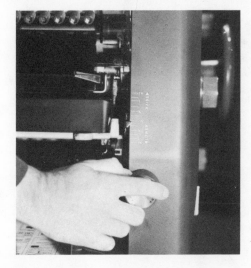

Fig. 9-10. Turn adjusting knob to raise or lower image on the sheet.

feeder if left and right-hand margins are not right.

11. Check ink coverage for a good printed image. Adjust ink coverage as shown in Fig. 9-11.

12. Set the counter, Fig. 9-12, and run the job.

Fig. 9-8. Tail of image carrier is attached to the cylinder.

Fig. 9-11. Ink flow from fountain to rollers is adjusted by turning thumbscrews called "keys."

Fig. 9-12. Setting the counter. This controls number of copies that will be printed.

All printing controls on the A.B. Dick 310 press are adjusted on the print control knob shown in Fig. 9-13. What happens to the press in each of the knob positions is shown in Fig. 9-14.

Control of the dampening solution is in the knob marked "Aquamatic Control." See Fig. 9-15.

After the printing job is finished, remove the printed stock from the delivery rack. Place the stock on a drying rack.

CLEANING THE PRESS

The press should be cleaned immediately after use.

1. Remove ink from the fountain. Do not return it to the same can.
2. Remove the ink fountain.
3. Drain remaining solution from the solution fountain. This need be done only weekly on the A.B. Dick 310.

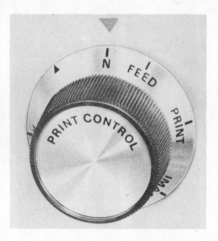

Fig. 9-13. Print control knob has seven different settings.

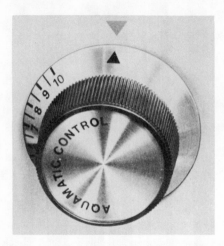

Fig. 9-15. Fountain solution being released to the rollers is controlled by this knob. (A.B. Dick Co.)

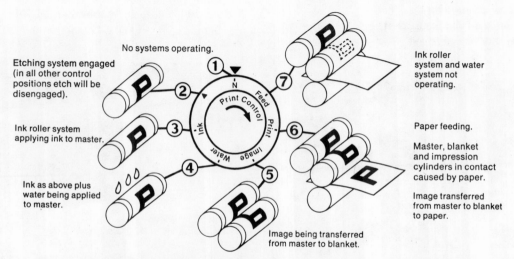

No systems operating.

Etching system engaged (in all other control positions etch will be disengaged).

Ink roller system applying ink to master.

Ink as above plus water being applied to master.

Image being transferred from master to blanket.

Ink roller system and water system not operating.

Paper feeding.

Master, blanket and impression cylinders in contact caused by paper.

Image transferred from master to blanket to paper.

Fig. 9-14. Various control knob positions and what happens when the knob is in each position.

Fig. 9-16. Industrial size press has more controls than table top models and can print a larger sheet size. (Heidelberg)

4. Remove the printing plate.
5. Attach the cleanup unit.
6. Operate press on low speed and apply cleanup solution. This step may need to be repeated several times to clean the rollers.
7. Clean the edges of the rollers and around the press with a cloth dampened with cleanup solution. CAUTION: Press must be stopped during this operation!
8. Clean the image from the blanket cylinder by holding down the ink cleanup lever indicated in Fig. 9-3.

LARGER OFFSET PRESSES

Becoming familiar with a small press, such as the one just described will help you understand the operation of large presses. Fig. 9-16 shows a sheet fed single color offset press. A four color press is seen in Fig. 9-17.

Fig. 9-18. This platen press is hand fed and power operated. (Chandler & Price Co.)

RELIEF (LETTERPRESS) PRESSWORK

Relief printing, also called letterpress, transfers ink from a raised surface. The substrate (material to be printed) is usually paper. With equipment found in the school laboratory, the typeform can be used as the image carrier. The form is locked in the chase as explained in Unit 8. Next it is secured to the bed of the press.

THE PLATEN PRESS

The PLATEN press takes its name from the flat metal platen or plate that holds the paper while it is

Fig. 9-17. Sheet fed four color press has four separate cylinder and inking systems.

being pressed against the image carrier. See Fig. 9-18 and Fig. 9-19.

Ink rollers of the platen press pass over the ink disc to pick up ink. Next, they roll over the form to ink the type.

While this operation is taking place, the operator or a mechanical feeder picks up a sheet of paper from the feed table and places it in the press. The paper is pressed against the inked form. When the press opens

Fig. 9-20. Operator uses ink knife to transfer ink from can to press.

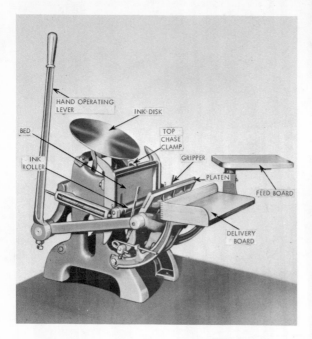

Fig. 9-19. Small platen presses are operated by hand.

up again, the printed sheet is removed and another takes it place. The printed sheet is placed on the delivery board.

PRESS PREPARATION

1. Apply a small amount of ink to the lower left-hand edge of the ink disc before placing the form in the press. See Fig. 9-20.
2. Operate the press to allow the rollers to distribute the ink evenly over the disc.
3. Stop the press with the rollers in the lowest position.
4. Dress the platen, Fig. 9-21. Lift the bails. These are the metal clamps that hold the packing on the platen. Place the following materials on the platen:
   a. One pressboard of smooth-finished hardboard, .020 in. (0.51 mm) thick.

Fig. 9-21. Dressing for the platen includes four layers of paper and a smooth-surfaced board.

   b. Three hanger sheets of about the thickness of 60 lb. and sc (supercalendered) book paper. This is a hard-finished paper sized and supercalendered to a smooth surface.
   c. An oiled manila tympan sheet .006 in. (0.152 mm) thick.
5. Clamp the tympan and hanger sheets under the bottom and top bails. Do not place the pressboard

under the bails.

6. Place the chase containing the image carrier (type-form) in the press and secure it with the clamps as shown in Fig. 9-22.

SETTING THE GRIPPERS

1. Sight across the gripers to make sure they will clear the form. Grippers are the fingers which close against the platen when the press closes. Their

Fig. 9-22. Bottom of chase is set against the two chase hooks; top is fastened with a chase clamp.

purpose is to hold the sheet flat against the tympan during the impression.

2. Reset the grippers if needed.

SETTING GAUGE PINS

Gauge pins are clips that hold the edges of the sheet while it is being printed. They must be properly located on the tympan sheet.

1. While turning the press slowly by hand, pull the throw-off lever toward you. This places the press on impression and an imprint will be left on the tympan sheet.

2. Find the position of the paper on the tympan. When the form is to be centered on the sheet:

   a. Place the edge of the sheet alongside the printed impression on the tympan. Line up left-hand edge with first line of type. Place a pencil mark, Fig. 9-23, on the sheet marking the last line.

   b. Fold the right-hand edge of the sheet up to the

Fig. 9-23. Method of centering form on the printed sheet. Divide distance below pencil mark by folding bottom edge to pencil mark.

pencil mark and crease it.

   c. Move the folded edge to align with the bottom line and mark the top margin. Unfold the bottom of the paper and mark the bottom margin. Draw guidelines top and bottom on the tympan.

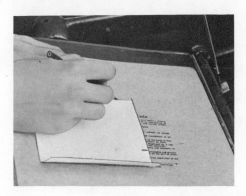

Fig. 9-24. To find top and bottom margin, place fold on last line of type; draw a guide line on tympan sheet along top and bottom edges of sheet.

   d. Repeat steps, a, b and c to mark remaining margins.

   e. If image is not being centered on the sheet, measure the distance with a rule and draw guidelines.

3. Fasten gauge pins to the tympan sheet, Fig. 9-25. Place two pins at the bottom of the tympan sheet about one-sixth the width of the paper from each edge. Place another pin on the left side of the tympan sheet about one-third the width of the sheet up from the bottom. Pins should be inserted as shown in Fig. 9-26.

4. Wipe the inked image off the tympan sheet. Use a clean rag moistened with solvent.

5. Make a trial impression operating the press by

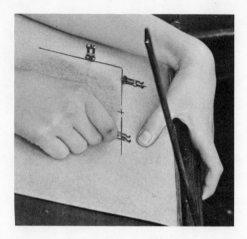

Fig. 9-25. Holes for gauge pins should be about 1/4 in. outside the guidelines.

Fig. 9-26. Position gauge pins as shown. End of prong must come back out of the tympan sheet so the pin cannot slip.

Fig. 9-27. Sheet is positioned in the gauge pins and impression is made to check accuracy of pin positions.

hand, Fig. 9-27.

6. Examine trial impression and adjust gauge pins if necessary.
7. When gauge pins are correctly positioned, set the pins by tapping them lightly with the press wrench, Fig. 9-28.

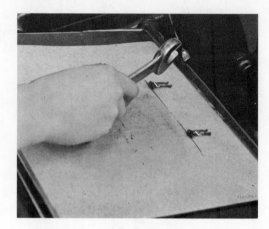

Fig. 9-28. Pins are tapped lightly to set them in the tympan sheet.

PRESS MAKE-READY

You will notice that some lines and letters do not print as heavily as others on the trial impression. This is normal and indicates the need for an operation called MAKE-READY. It is the term used for making an overlay sheet that will be placed in the packing. It creates additional thickness so that light areas will print darker. To prepare a make-ready sheet:

1. Place carbon paper upside down under a trial print.
2. Circle areas on proof that seem to be too light, Fig. 9-29. Very light areas may need additional buildup. Draw a second circle around these. They will need additional thickness of paper.
3. Turn sheet over and apply make-ready paste to the circled areas. First apply the tissue to areas needing more than one thickness of paper.
4. Lay pieces of make-ready tissue over each area and cut them to shape of the area with a make-ready knife.
5. Place the overlay sheet in the press against the guides.
6. With the make-ready knife, stab the sheet along the right side making two carets (upside down "Vs"). Press hard enough to cut through the tympan sheet and into the first hanger sheet. See Fig. 9-30.

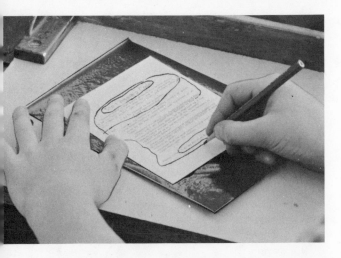

Fig. 9-29. Circling print areas where ink is too light is called "marking out."

Fig. 9-30. Stab overlay to make register marks in the packing.

7. Raise top bail and fold back tympan sheet.
8. Attach the make-ready sheet to the top hanger sheet. Line up the caret cuts before pasting the sheet down, Fig. 9-31.
9. Remove the pressboard from the bottom of the packing and place it between the tympan sheet and the hanger sheet which has the overlay make-ready sheet attached to it. This provides a firmer impression surface and causes less wear on the type.

Fig. 9-31. Attach make-ready sheet to top hanger sheet.

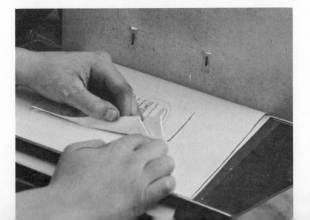

10. Replace the tympan sheet and the bail.
11. Take a second trial impression.
12. If the impression shows too much punch (type presses into printed sheet), remove one of the lower hanger sheets. If the impression is still too light, add an additional sheet to the packing.
13. When make-ready is completed, position the grippers so they will help hold the sheet against the pins. Place them in the margins where they will not strike the type. See Fig. 9-32.

Fig. 9-32. Grippers, properly positioned, will not strike the type. Note use of gripper fingers.

FEEDING THE PRESS

1. Place paper stock on the feedboard. Fan the sheets so you can pick up one sheet at a time.
2. Set the counter by turning all the number wheels to nine. The first impression will trip the numbers to zero.
3. Turn on the power and run the press slowly.
4. Feed the press with the right-hand and remove the sheets with the left, Fig. 9-33. If for any reason you do not wish to make the impression, push the throw-off lever forward. Press will not print in this position.

Fig. 9-33. Proper method for hand feeding the press.

SAMMY SAFETY SAYS:

"Remember there must be only one operator at the press. Keep your hands out of the press when it is making the impression. Make sure the grippers are not in the way of the type. . .the form will be smashed. Put all soiled rags in a closed metal container."

CLEANING THE PLATEN PRESS

If ink is allowed to dry on the ink disc and rollers, the press may be damaged. It should be cleaned immediately after the printing job is completed.

1. Remove the chase and place it on the stone.
2. Wash off the typeform using a cloth dampened with cleaning solvent.
3. Store the chase until you can distribute the type.
4. Moisten a cloth with solvent and clean the ink from the ink disc.
5. Turn the press slowly by hand until the rollers are at the lower edge of the ink disc, Fig. 9-34.
6. Clean off each roller, turning the press by hand to expose the entire surface of each roller. Remove all ink including the ends.
7. Reclean the ink disc.
8. Turn rollers back to the lowest position.

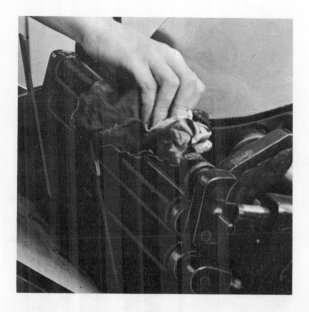

Fig. 9-34. With rollers just below ink disc, cleaning of the press begins.

CAUTION: Place soiled rags in a closed metal container to avoid danger of fire.

SPECIAL PRINTING OPERATIONS

The platen press can be used for special jobs that do not involve putting ink on the material to be printed. These operations include:

1. Scoring or creasing.
2. Perforating.
3. Die cutting.
4. Numbering.
5. Thermography.

SCORING OR CREASING

Scoring or creasing makes folding of heavy paper easier. The scoring rule is made of special steel that is tough and long wearing. The edge striking the paper is rounded to avoid cutting the paper. Most jobs are scored with the rollers removed.

PERFORATING

The perforating rule is shaped to cut small slits in the paper so it will tear more easily. Perforating can be performed during printing or as a separate operation. It is common to save a set of old rollers to use for this task.

DIE CUTTING

In die cutting, paper is cut to special shapes. Most dies are purchased already formed. The die is locked up in the case in the same way as a typeform. The rollers are removed and a piece of sheet metal is placed beneath the draw sheet on the platen.

NUMBERING

When tickets or other material must be numbered, a numbering device is locked up with the form. Each time an impression is made, the number advances.

THERMOGRAPHY

In thermography, the job is printed in the normal way. But, before the ink has dried, a powder or compound is spread on the sheet. The excess is removed. What remains, sticks to the ink. The sheet is heated and the powder fuses. The effect is a raised kind of printing that looks like engraving.

Fig. 9-35. Automatic platen press is used in industry.

COMMERCIAL PRESSES

The basics of presswork, learned on small equipment just described, can be applied to large industrial letterpress equipment. Fig. 9-35 shows a high speed automatic platen press. Fig. 9-36 shows a web press used to print newspapers.

SCREEN PROCESS
IMAGE TRANSFER

In the silk-screen process, the image is transferred when the ink is forced through a design or stencil and contacts the substrate surface. The device holding the image carrier can be a simple homemade frame. See Fig. 9-37.

Fig. 9-37. Three basic tools for silk screen printing are frame, screen and squeegee.

ATTACHING IMAGE CARRIER

1. Assemble the materials needed: adhering liquid, masking tape, wrapping paper, wrapping tape, rags and lacquer thinner.
2. Place the original copy on the screen board.
3. Set the guides so the sheets will be fed at the proper position.
4. Position the cut stencil (image carrier) in register over the design and tape it only at the corners, Fig. 9-38.
5. Lower the screen over the stencil.

Fig. 9-38. Pieces of chipboard fastened to the base of the screen frame serve as guides for printing stock.

Fig. 9-36. Goss headliner press installed for newspaper work. (Chicago Sun Times)

Fig. 9-39. Film is positioned on the silkscreen and temporarily fastened to the base with tape.

6. Use two rags to adhere the stencil. Saturate one with adhering liquid and rub over a small portion of the stencil. Quickly wipe area with a dry rag.
7. Remove the original copy and tape from the stencil.
8. Place several layers of newsprint under the stencil.
9. Adhere rest of the stencil alternating short strokes with the damp and dry rags. CAUTION: Too much adhering liquid can destroy the stencil. Work carefully and pick up excess liquid immediately with the dry rag, Fig. 9-39.
10. While the stencil is drying, cut a piece of wrapping paper to the size of the screen. Cut out the center so that it frames the stencil. Tape it to the upper side of the silk screen. Use masking tape around the stencil and wrapping tape around the screen frame. This will block out the non-image area around the stencil so it will not print, and is suitable for short runs.
11. For longer runs, use a special block-out solution. This material is squeegeed over all areas of the screen that should not print.

Fig. 9-40. Apply adhering liquid with short brushing strokes of the solvent saturated rags. Wipe the area stroked immediately with a dry cloth. Too much solvent could damage the emulsion.

12. When the stencil is dry, remove the backing material, Fig. 9-40. The stencil is then ready for printing.

PRINTING BY SILK SCREEN

1. Place a sheet of paper in the guides.
2. Lower the stencil over the sheet of paper.
3. Place a ribbon of silk screen ink in the frame near the hinged top, the width of the image.
4. Using the squeegee, pull the ink across the image as shown in Fig. 9-41.

Fig. 9-41. Press firmly on squeegee and drag it across image. Ink will be pushed through holes of screen onto paper underneath.

5. Use the squeegee to lift the excess ink and transfer it to the hinge side of the frame.
6. Lift the frame, remove the print and inspect it for flaws.
7. Repeat process for every additional printed sheet.
8. Stack printed sheets separately on drying rack.

SCREEN CLEANUP

1. Using a piece of chipboard, remove ink from the screen and squeegee.
2. Clean off ink with rags and solvent.
3. Remove and discard block-out paper. Special block-out material can be reused if the stencil is to be used again.

REMOVING IMAGE CARRIER

If no additional prints will be made from the stencil, it can be washed out using the following procedure. For removing a lacquer stencil:

1. Pour a small amount of lacquer thinner over the stencil area. (Use newspapers under the stencil to soak up solvent.)
2. Cover the stencil with newsprint and let stand for about 5 minutes. Lacquer thinner will dissolve most of the stencil.

Fig. 9-42. Lacquer thinner and rags are used to remove lacquer film from screen.

3. When layers of newspaper are removed, most of the stencil materials will be gone.
4. With two solvent soaked rags, rub both sides for final cleaning, Fig. 9-42.
5. If block-out solution was used, wash it out with hot water. Screen should then be ready for storage or reuse.

ADHERING PHOTO STENCILS

Stencils made by the photographic method must be adhered to the screen immediately after it is washed out.

1. Place the wet stencil under the screen in register with the original. Emulsion side should be up.
2. Use blotting paper or newsprint and press lightly on the screen to help adhere emulsion to screen.
3. Stand the frame up to allow the screen and film to dry thoroughly.
4. Peel off the emulsion support.
5. Mask screen as described for lacquer stencil.

Clean up procedure is the same as for a lacquer stencil. To remove the stencil, soak or spray it with hot water, Fig. 9-43.

Fig. 9-43. Spraying or soaking with hot water removes water soluble photo stencil.

INTAGLIO OR GRAVURE PRESSWORK

Basic principles of the intaglio printing process are illustrated in Unit 6. There are no gravure presses in school laboratories but industry uses some rather large gravure units, Fig. 9-44.

QUIZ — UNIT 9

1. Name the six systems found on a lithographic press.
2. Never wear _____ clothing around a press.
3. How many pieces and what kind of material is used in dressing a platen press?
4. Decorative cutting of a sheet of paper on the press is called _____.
5. The image carrier in a silk screen operation is called a _____.
6. In silk screening, the image carrier is removed with either _____ _____ or _____ _____.

Fig. 9-44. Industry uses large rotogravure presses.   (Champlain Co.)

BINDING AND FINISHING OPERATIONS

1. Finishing operations which give printed matter its final form.
2. Operations that cut and shape printed matter.
3. Operations that gather, fasten, enclose or protect printed matter.

Binding and finishing operations include everything that is done to the shape of the final printed piece after it comes from the printing press. It includes also the things that are done to keep the pages of the product fastened together or to protect them. These operations are known as:

1. Cutting and trimming.
2. Punching.
3. Perforating.
4. Drilling.
5. Collating.
6. Padding.
7. Stitching.
8. Binding.
9. Wrapping.

These operations take place in a section of the pressroom or in a separate room. This section or room is called the BINDERY. While most of the operations take place after the piece is printed, cutting may be done before the material is placed on the press. Large press sheets secured from the supply house often must be cut to press size.

SAMMY SAFETY
SAYS:

"Handle tools and equipment in the bindery with great care. Follow these safety rules."

1. Secure permission from the instructor before using the paper cutter, hot stamp press, wire stitcher or other power equipment.
2. Never wear jewelry or wrist watches while operating equipment with moving parts. Tie back long hair where it cannot become entangled in moving parts.

3. When operating the paper cutter, make sure no one else is inside the operator's safety zone. After each cut, check to see that the knife lever which controls the blade is in the "up" position and securely locked with the knife safety button, pin or lever. Keep hands clear of the blade at all times. Limit amount of stock being cut at any one time. If safety devices do not require the use of both hands during cutting, keep them on the lever. See that the lever is in the proper position with safety lock engaged before adjusting position of the back gage.
4. Never point hand shears at classmates. Carry them with the blades pointing backward and downward.
5. Keep hands from under the head of the wire stitcher and make sure head is clear before turning on the machine. Wear safety glasses.
6. Use the hot stamp machine with caution to avoid burning the hands.
7. Keep glue pots clean. Set them where they cannot be accidently tipped.
8. Keep fingers and hands away from the jaws of the clamping press.
9. Keep knives and saws sharp. Handle them carefully to avoid injury.
10. Store pointed instruments carefully and exercise care in their use.

PAPER CUTTING

Paper cutting is, perhaps, the most common of the bindery operations. A hand-lever cutter is shown in Fig. 10-1. It is often found in small commercial shops as well as in graphic arts laboratories in schools.

A large, power-operated cutter is shown in Fig. 10-2. Similar units are found in commercial shops.

OPERATING HAND-LEVER CUTTERS

To operate a cutter as shown in Fig. 10-3, load the paper stock onto the cutter table. Jog it first to even up the edges. Slide the stock against a metal bar at the back of the cutter. This bar is called a BACK GAGE. Sometimes it is called the "back fence." It can be moved backward or forward for width by turning the handwheel under the cutting table.

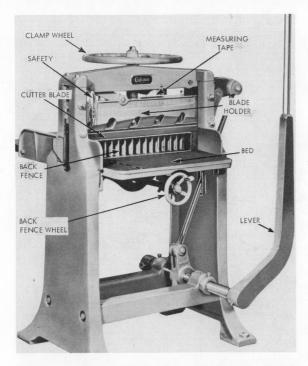

Fig. 10-1. Hand-lever paper cutter. Swinging lever to left causes cutter blade to descend and cut through stack of paper. (Chandler & Price Co.)

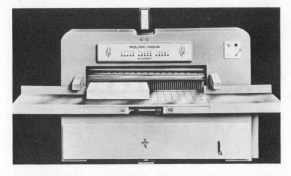

Fig. 10-2. Single-knife hydraulic paper cutter is powered by electric motors. It is accurate to .001 in. (.025 mm). (Heidelberg Eastern, Inc.)

Fig. 10-3. A lift of paper must be jogged before being placed in the cutter.

On some cutters, a metal tape travels with the back gage to register the depth of cut. On other cutters, a ruler or yardstick is used for measuring.

After the depth of cut is set, lock the handwheel with a THUMBSCREW. Turn the handwheel at the top of the cutter to bring down the CLAMP. This is a movable bar that holds the paper in place while the cut is made.

To keep the paper from being marred by the clamp, and to assure a clean cut on the bottom sheets, place pieces of cardboard on top and underneath the stack (lift) of paper.

Grasp the knife lever with the right hand. Pull the knife safety with the left hand, as in Fig. 10-4. Lower the knife a little to release the safety. Bring the knife to the paper and then pull the lever firmly to carry the knife through the stack.

Fig. 10-4. Operating paper cutter. Left-hand is being used to release the safety device.

PAPER FOLDING

Most binderies have machines that will fold the sheets many different ways, Fig. 10-5. Small commercial printers and school laboratories have friction feed folders as shown in Fig. 10-6. Larger commercial shops have more complex folding machines as in Fig. 10-7. Folders accomplish the folding operation in two ways. The first of these is the knife type folder. Fig. 10-8 shows how it works. This is a very accurate folding device used with large printed sheets.

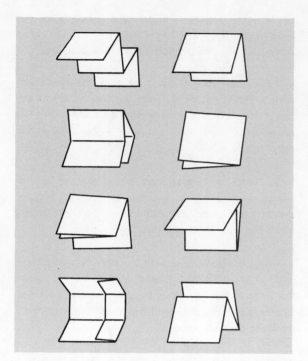

Fig. 10-5. Machines can be set to make any of these basic folds.

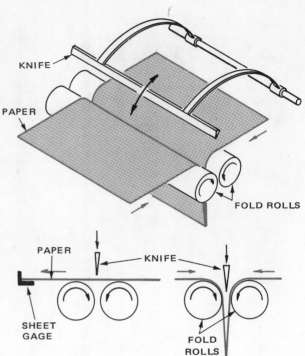

Fig. 10-8. Knife type folder depends on overhead blade to start fold. It pushes down on middle of sheet until it is caught and pulled through the rollers.

Fig. 10-6. Simple friction feed folder being used to make one fold in 11 by 17 in. sheet.

The buckle type folder, shown in Fig. 10-9 is the most popular of the folding devices. It is the type of action used in the small friction feed folders.

All folders consist of a feeder, registration and conveyor system. The folding unit can be adjusted to make different kinds of folds.

In the school graphic arts laboratory, simple folding may be done with a bone folder as shown in Fig. 10-10.

PERFORATING AND SCORING

Some folding machines have special detachable wheels that perforate and score. See Fig. 10-11.

Perforating is the process of cutting or punching small slits or holes into the sheets so that the two parts can be separated easily. Scoring puts a dent across the sheet so that it can be folded accurately. Fig. 10-12 shows a scored and perforated job.

PADDING

In PADDING operations, special adhesive is placed on one edge of a stack of paper sheets to hold them

Fig. 10-7. Large folder can make several folds and handle larger sheets. (Heidelberg Eastern, Inc.)

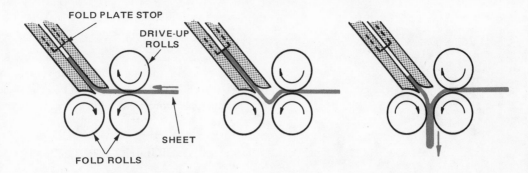

Fig. 10-9. Buckle folder uses a stop and an extra roller to make a fold.

Fig. 10-10 Bone folder is used to make fold in sheet of paper.

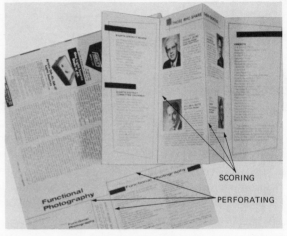

Fig. 10-12. These printed pieces were perforated and scored on a folding machine.

Fig. 10-11. Detachable wheels for folding machine. Notched wheel at left is for perforating; smooth ring at right is used to score the sheet so it will fold neatly.

Fig. 10-13. Special padding adhesive is applied by brush to sheets as they are clamped tightly in a padding press.

together as a pad. The paper is jogged to make the ends square. A piece of chipboard is placed at the bottom of the pile. Then the whole unit is placed in a padding press. Usually several units are padded at once, as shown in Fig. 10-13.

Fig. 10-14. This machine quickly collates and side stitches up to 1000 booklets an hour. (Pitney Bowes, Inc.)

COLLATING

Gathering parts of a job in a regular sequence, such as the pages of a booklet, is called COLLATING. This is often done before the binding operation. Large binderies collate with automatic equipment. See Figs. 10-14 and 10-15.

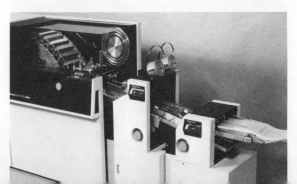

Fig. 10-15. Bin collator collects sheets stored in the bins and places them in page order. (Pitney Bowes, Inc.)

DRILLING AND PUNCHING

DRILLING and PUNCHING operations make holes in paper to be bound into a unit by mechanical fasteners. The fastener may be a ring binder, metal or plastic device.

Heavy-duty punching equipment uses pressure to push a die through a stack of sheets. The holes can be round or any other shape to suit the fastener. A paper drill uses a twisting motion to cut holes through large stacks of paper.

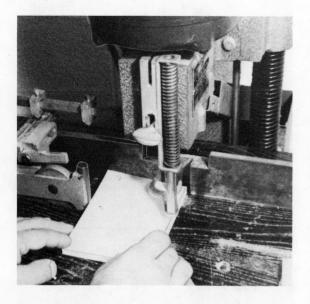

Fig. 10-16. Paper drill works like a drill press. Cutting is done with a twisting motion of the drill bit.

The special paper drill in Fig. 10-16 makes holes in paper stacks to fit various notebooks or bindings. Paper drills with multiple heads can cut several holes as one operation, Fig. 10-17.

BINDING OPERATIONS

BINDING includes all the ways of fastening pages together. Often, this includes a cover. Fig. 10-18 shows some of the methods used. Most magazines and small pamphlets are held with wire staples. Some are SADDLE STITCHED; others are SIDE STITCHED.

Books with hard covers are usually case bound. Paper or soft covered books may be side stitched, saddle stitched, or glued with a flexible adhesive.

Fig. 10-17. Multiple head paper drill can cut several holes at once.

STITCHING AND STAPLING

STITCHING and STAPLING both hold several sheets together with short pieces of wire. The stitcher in Fig. 10-19, is fed wire from a roll. It cuts and shapes its own staples. The staple machine uses preformed staples.

Staples are attached to the sheets in two different ways. In the side-wire binding, Fig. 10-20, the staples are inserted in the left-hand edge or margin. In saddle-wire binding, the staples are inserted through the fold. See Fig. 10-21.

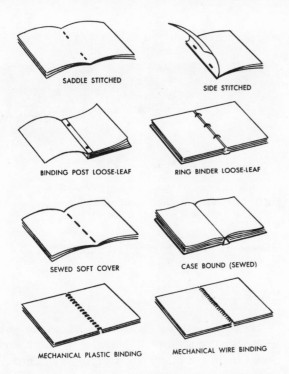

SADDLE STITCHED   SIDE STITCHED

BINDING POST LOOSE-LEAF   RING BINDER LOOSE-LEAF

SEWED SOFT COVER   CASE BOUND (SEWED)

MECHANICAL PLASTIC BINDING   MECHANICAL WIRE BINDING

Fig. 10-18. Eight basic types of binding. Case binding is the most expensive.

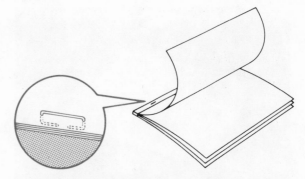

Fig. 10-20. Side-wire staples are pushed through the face of the booklet in the left-hand margin.

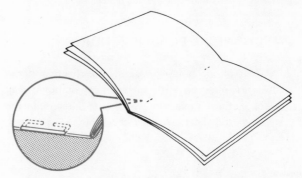

Fig. 10-21. In saddle stitching, staples are pushed through the fold into the center of the booklet.

Fig. 10-19. Saddle stitching is always done with a power operated machine.

High-production machines combine the collating and stitching operations in one unit. See Fig. 10-22.

PERFECT BINDING

The PERFECT BINDING process uses adhesive on the edges of the gathered sheets. A soft cover is also held by the adhesive. Paperback books (pocketbooks) are usually bound this way. Fig. 10-23 shows a small perfect binding machine and a perfect-bound book.

Fig. 10-22. Large machine gathers printed piece and stitches them. (Harris Corp.)

Fig. 10-23. Perfect binding operation trims and roughens the folded edges of sheets and applies a hot glue.

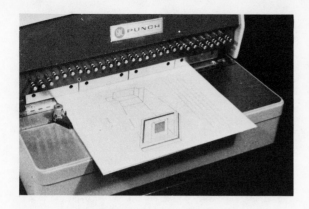

Fig. 10-24. This machine punches series of holes to receive fingers of a plastic binding.

Fig. 10-25. Second machine opens plastic binder and inserts "fingers" of binding through holes.

MECHANICAL PLASTIC BINDING

When plastic binding is used, the sheets and the cover are punched with special slots or holes. Fig. 10-24 pictures a machine which cuts the slots in the edges of the sheets. A second machine, Fig. 10-25,

attaches the plastic binder. This type binding allows the booklet to open flat.

CASE BINDING

Textbooks, library books, encyclopedias are known as CASE BOUND books. The case bound book is sewn and then a separate cover is attached to

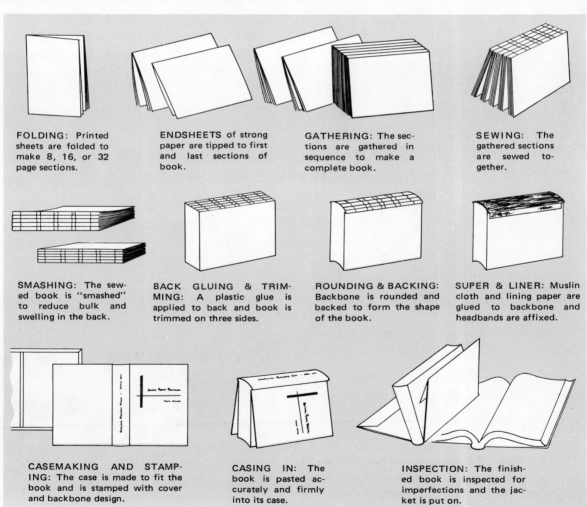

FOLDING: Printed sheets are folded to make 8, 16, or 32 page sections.

ENDSHEETS of strong paper are tipped to first and last sections of book.

GATHERING: The sections are gathered in sequence to make a complete book.

SEWING: The gathered sections are sewed together.

SMASHING: The sewed book is "smashed" to reduce bulk and swelling in the back.

BACK GLUING & TRIMMING: A plastic glue is applied to back and book is trimmed on three sides.

ROUNDING & BACKING: Backbone is rounded and backed to form the shape of the book.

SUPER & LINER: Muslin cloth and lining paper are glued to backbone and headbands are affixed.

CASEMAKING AND STAMPING: The case is made to fit the book and is stamped with cover and backbone design.

CASING IN: The book is pasted accurately and firmly into its case.

INSPECTION: The finished book is inspected for imperfections and the jacket is put on.

Fig. 10-26. Major steps in case binding of books. (John F. Cuneo Co.)

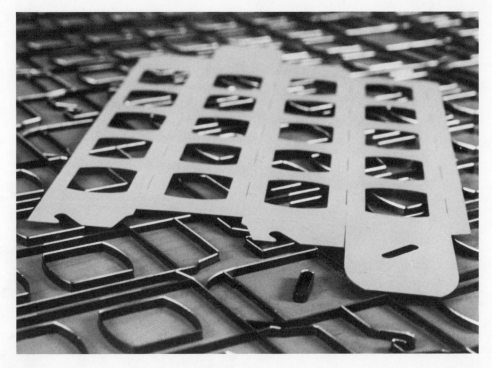

Fig. 10-27. A die cut "pest strip" carton and the commercial die which produced it.   (Atlas Steel Rule Die, Inc.)

it. The cover and the book are glued together in a casing-in machine. The major steps in case binding are shown in Fig. 10-26.

DIE CUTTING

While the die cutting operation is usually performed with press equipment, it is considered a finishing process. Fig. 10-27 shows a commercial die used; in the carton and container industry.

QUIZ — UNIT 10

1. List the nine different operations in binding and finishing.
2. In cutting paper, the rear guide against which the stock is placed is called the _____ _____.
3. All folders have the three following basic systems:
   a. Conveyor system.
   b. Bone folder.
   c. Feeder.
   d. Registration system.
   e. Perforator.
4. Punching small slits or holes in the sheets is called _____; putting a dent across the sheets is called _____.
5. Putting sheets in page order before fastening them together is called:
   a. Binding.
   b. Collating.
   c. Padding.
   d. Pagination.

PAPER, INK AND OTHER MATERIALS

UNIT 11

1. How printing paper is made.
2. Kinds of printing paper.
3. Basic sizes and weights of paper.
4. Manufacturing inks and other printing materials.

Paper and ink are the two main ingredients in the making of printed products. Printing is done on other materials besides paper. Metal, plastic and woven materials are also used.

Inks are specially designed to meet the needs of various printing processes.

Besides these two major ingredients, modern graphic arts processes require printing plates made of both metal and synthetic materials, photographic films, chemicals, solvents, adhesives, tapes and special powders.

THE MAKING OF PAPER

The process of making paper was first discovered in China in the year 105 A.D. by a man named Ts'ai Lun. Like so many of our technologies, it began as a hand process and developed into a manufacturing science.

Paper is divided into types according to its method of manufacture:

1. Ground wood (mechanical) pulp.
2. Chemical pulp.
3. Semi-chemical pulp.

Pulp is the major substance from which paper is made. The raw material for the pulp comes from trees (wood pulp), cotton and linen (rag pulp). Fig. 11-1 shows logs ready for the papermaking process.

Through grinding or chemical action, Fig. 11-2, the solid material is changed to a pulp state and is thinned with water. The pulp, is spread over a large screen in a thin layer. The screen is called a

Fig. 11-1. Most papermaking fiber comes from wood. Logs are stored at the paper mill until they can be processed.

Fig. 11-2. Logs are reduced to chips which are moved by conveyors to continue the process of breaking down the wood to fibers.

FOURDRINIER WIRE. It is part of a large machine. See Fig. 11-3. The pulp is formed into paper while the screen section of the machine moves along like a conveyor. In the first stage of manufacture, the paper pulp loses most of its water content. The second stage of the process presses the sheet to a desired thickness and removes more of the water.

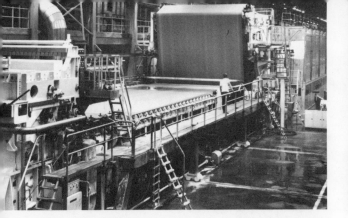

Fig. 11-3. The papermaking machine is called a Fourdrinier. This one is computer controlled. The screen can move at 2000 feet per minute. (The Mead Corp.)

Fig. 11-5. A 110 in. guillotine trimmer cuts paper into different sheet sizes.

The paper becomes a continuous web as it moves along the Fourdrinier machine. One section of the machine dries the web of paper. Then the paper passes between highly polished cylinders called CALENDER ROLLERS where it is polished and smoothed. Finally, it is stored on a larger roller to await further processing.

Quality control is essential in the making of the paper. Sensitive instruments check the paper continuously. See Fig. 11-4.

Fig. 11-4. Computers help take over the work of checking color, density and uniformity of paper as it is being made. Computer keeps track of some 135 instrument readings. (The Mead Corp.)

CONVERTING AND FINISHING

Further processing is called paper CONVERTING and FINISHING. The large roll may be cut into smaller (narrower) rolls for web press printing. Some paper passes through embossing rolls for special finishes. Other large rolls are fed into the machines that trim them into sheets for sheet-fed presses. Fig. 11-5 shows the trimming operation. A general over-view of the entire papermaking process is shown in Fig. 11-6.

KINDS OF PAPER

Printing papers come in a great variety of types, weights, textures, colors and prices. It is important for the printers to know about the various kinds so they can select the right paper for the job. Paper is chosen before the job is planned so that all of the processes will be compatible to the type of stock chosen. The type faces used, the printing process, the press and ink must be right for the paper.

Each manufacturer of paper has a slightly different system of classifying paper. You will use a general grouping in this text.

NEWSPRINT

Newsprint paper is, as the name suggests, used for printing newspapers and handbills. It is an inexpensive paper made from ground wood pulp.

BOOK PAPERS

Book papers are made in many different weights and finishes. Some papers are soft and porous; some are the finest grades of smooth, coated paper. Book papers are used for printing books, magazines, catalogs, programs and pamphlets. Among the different kinds are the following:

1. Machine finished book. An inexpensive book paper, it is a better grade of paper than newsprint.
2. Supercalendered book. A sized paper, it will not absorb ink. It is a better grade than machine finished paper.
3. Sized and supercalendered paper is like a supercalendered paper but has a harder finish. It is better for printing halftones or pictures.

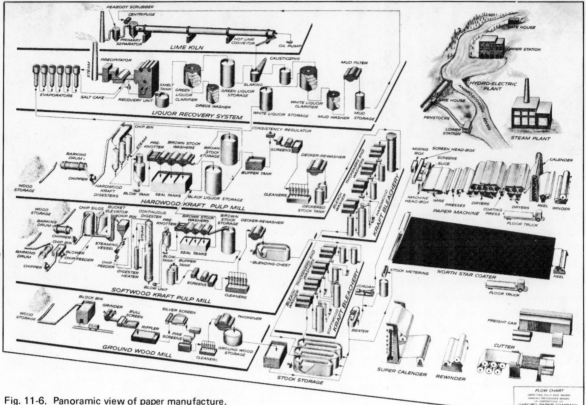

Fig. 11-6. Panoramic view of paper manufacture.

4. Coated enamel papers are used for reproducing fine halftone work.
5. Offset paper is specially made for the offset process. It is water resistant.
6. Antique paper is a bulky, soft, porous paper. It is used chiefly for books where no illustrations are necessary. It is also used for programs.
7. English finished paper resembles the antique paper but is smoother and less bulky.

WRITING PAPERS

Known as bonds, ledgers and mineograph bonds, writing papers are made to be used with ink, pencil and printing inks. Some writing papers contain rag fibers. These are called rag content papers.

CARDBOARDS

Cardboards are thick, stiff papers used for ticket stock, file cards and poster paper. They have different names, characteristics and uses.

1. Index and printing bristols are used for printing jobs requiring stiffness. They are designed for use as die-cut items, tickets and file cards.
2. Railroad board is a heavy stock used for tickets, pamphlets and book covers.
3. Chipboard is an inexpensive gray-colored board used on the backs of tablets.

COVER PAPERS

Cover papers are thicker than book papers but not as thick as cardboards. They come in many finishes such as: ripple, laid, coated and plate. They are used for covers, menus, bulletins and catalogs.

MISCELLANEOUS PAPERS

Other papers fall into the miscellaneous class. These include:

1. Gummed papers with glue coating on one side.
2. Thin papers used for second sheets and air mail letters.
3. Blotter stock which is a thick absorbent sheet.

BASIC SIZES AND WEIGHTS

A ream or 500 sheets of paper is the weight standard for paper used by printers. Paper comes in many different stock sizes and in a number of different weights. Special sizes are made to order. Each type of paper stock has a different BASIC size. Let us see what we mean by that statement. When we speak of 70 lb. book stock, it means that 500 sheets of this paper, in size 25 x 38, weigh 70 lb. The basic size is 25 x 38. When we refer to a 28 lb. bond, it means that 500 sheets of this paper, 17 x 22 in size, weigh 28 lb.

The table, Fig. 11-7, will enable you to tell at a glance, the comparative weights of different types of stock. You will note that a 70 lb. book stock, a 38 lb. cover and a 28 lb. bond, are all about the same weight and thickness.

METRIC SIZES AND WEIGHTS (MASS)

In countries that have gone metric there are two series of sizes, the A series and the B series. Eventually, the United States, too, will adopt these sizes. They are referred to as the ISO paper sizes. The A series is the main one used for general printing. It is based on the AO size which is a sheet measuring 841 millimetres by 1 189 millimetres. Its total area is 1 square metre (1 m^2). The largest size in the A series is 2A which is twice the AO size. Each smaller size is half the next larger size.

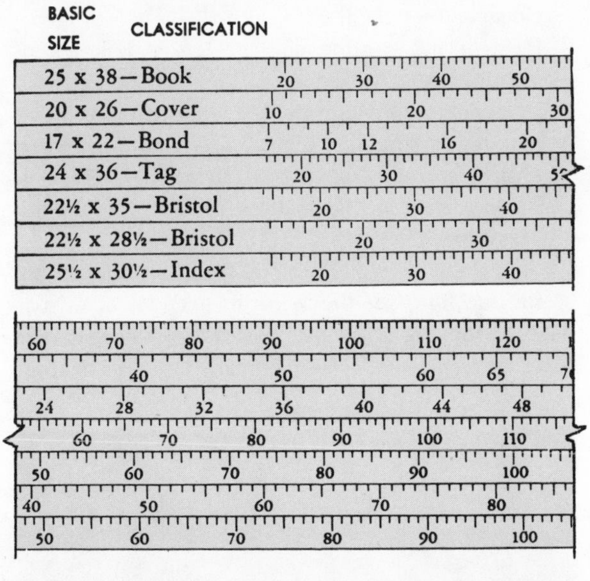

Fig. 11-7. Weights of different kinds of papers. To compare, find numbers from different papers that align vertically. For example, weight of a 20 lb. book paper is about the same per sheet as 11 lb. cover.   (James White Paper Co.)

The B series is used for posters and wall charts. The BO size measures 1 000 by 1 414 millimetres. It is larger than the AO size.

In metric, weight is referred to as MASS. The basic mass of paper is expressed in grams per square metre (g/m^2) of a single sheet. This is different from our customary method which is to give the weight of 500 sheets. To convert from pounds per ream to grams per square metre, it is necessary to use a conversion factor. Usually there are charts for this purpose.

PROPERTIES OF FINISHED PAPERS

Papers have certain properties. It is important that the printer know about these as they influence the way the paper is used:

1. Grain is the direction of the fibers in the finished sheet. Paper curls with the grain if it is subjected to moisture. It is best to fold paper with the grain and not across the grain. The printer needs to know this, especially when printing a book.
2. Finish is a term applied to the appearance of the paper. Some stock is coated. Some is smooth. Some has an embossed design and some has a soft or antique finish.
3. Density is the amount of air space between the fibers. It is also a term used when explaining the difference between high bulk papers and thin papers.
4. Brightness is the ability of the paper to reflect light.
5. Opacity is the ability of the paper to prevent passage of light through it. Opacity allows the printer to print on both sides of the sheet. Fibers of opaque papers are tightly woven.
6. Wire side/felt side refers to the right and wrong side of the sheet. The wire side is the underside of the sheet when the paper is formed. The felt side is smoother. However, modern manufacturing processes have minimized this effect and most papers are good on both sides.

PRINTING INKS

Printing ink is the second of the major ingredients in the manufacture of a printed job. Printing ink, like paper, was developed and used in China for block printing many years before the discovery of printing from movable type by Gutenberg.

Except for newspaper type inks, most inks are manufactured by what is known as the batch process. The news inks are a continuous line production. The batch making allows the ink manufacturer to customize the order for the printer to match the stock being used. The ingredients found in the ink are shown in Fig. 11-8.

Other ingredients impart special characteristics to the inks. These are usually driers, but also include waxes, lubricants, gums, starches and wetting agents. The driers, which are the main additives, are there to speed the drying process.

Fig. 11-8. Ink has several ingredients. Reading clockwise from extreme left. Vehicle, thinner, wax, resin and pigment.

Printing ink is essentially a mixture of a vehicle or varnish, pigment and drier. Fig. 11-9 shows a three-spindle mixer. The properties of ink can be controlled according to the type of printing and the press being used. In general, the basic requirements are:

1. Uniform consistency.
2. Viscosity (rate of flow) suited to the speed of the press and the rate at which it is to be applied.
3. Drying qualities to prevent smudging and to permit handling of the printed sheets within a reasonable time.

Inks are suited to the needs of the three major printing processes and the specialty printing processes. Inks can be grouped under seven basic types:

1. Letterpress inks are formulated to work with various kinds of paper and with the speeds of different presses. Fig. 11-10 shows a mixing operation in an ink mill.
2. Flexographic inks require special characteristics because they are applied to flexible and often glossy surfaces.
3. Lithographic inks must be resistant to emulsification (mixing with water) because of the moisture used in lithographic printing.
4. Gravure inks need to have special solvents and binders added to the ink to develop maximum adhesion to the printing surfaces.
5. Screen process inks are more like paint and are formulated to print through the screen without clogging the stencil.
6. Electrostatic printing, copper plate and die stamping also require special inks.
7. A recent technology called sublimation printing requires a special ink that will transfer printed images to cloth when heat is applied. This ink changes from a solid to a gas, then back to a solid. This allows the transfer of the design.

In addition to the general ink characteristics needed for the different processes, manufacturers make other inks with special characteristics: heat-set

Fig. 11-9. Special machines thoroughly mix the printing ink ingredients. (NAPIM)

Fig. 11-10. Three-roll mill grinds ink particles until extremely fine. Then it blends the particles with the vehicle (oil).

inks, moisture-set inks, quick-set inks, high gloss inks, metallic inks, wax-set inks, water color inks and cold-set inks.

Most inks are used right from the container. However, one of the major tasks of the small shop is to mix certain colors. Always start with the lightest color and add very small amounts of the darker color until the new color is right.

OFFSET PRINTING PLATES

Another important product used by the printer is the offset printing plate. It is fabricated from large rolls of aluminum as shown in Fig. 11-11. The metal is cut to size in special machines, Fig. 11-12. The plates are then grained, Fig. 11-13. Finally a coating of sensitized material is applied under a safelight.

Fig. 11-11. Huge roll of sheet aluminum ready to be processed into photo-offset plates.   (Western Litho Plate)

Fig. 11-12. Offset plates are cut to size in large production machines.   (Western Litho Plate)

Fig. 11-13. Grainer produces finish on offset plates before they are coated with sensitized material.

OTHER MATERIALS AND SUPPLIES

Other materials needed by the graphic arts industry are products which the customer never sees. They are used as aids in the manufacturing process. They include:

1. Photographic films and papers. These are used in both continuous tone and process photography.
2. Clear films, used in stripping operations.
3. Adhesive backed tape, used in negative assembly and stripping operations.
4. Adhesives, used in bindery operations.
5. Chemicals, used in photographic operations and in press fountain solutions.
6. Solvents, used in cleanup operations.
7. Lubricants, used for machine operation.
8. Special powders, used in heat printing (thermography) and for nonoffset sprays.

QUIZ — UNIT 11

1. The principal raw materials from which paper is made are _____ and _____.
2. List the six general types of paper used by the printing industry.
3. The basis weight of a sheet of paper is the weight of a _____ which is _____ sheets.
4. Metric weight or mass of paper is based on the weight of a _____ _____.
5. Name the six properties of finished papers.
6. The basic requirements of all inks used in printing are uniform consistency, _____ and _____ _____.

MATHEMATICS FOR PRINTERS

1. Printers' systems of measurement.
2. Measuring type and fitting copy.
3. Cutting paper.
4. Figuring costs of paper.
5. Scaling illustrations.

Printers must take many measurements and make many computations in the course of their work. The printing industry has always used the inch system and the point system. Now there is a move toward the metric system. When the changeover comes and printing becomes all metric, it most likely will be a "hard conversion." In other words, the old sizes will be abandoned and new sizes that fit metric units will be used. But for the present, the customary systems are still dominant.

Unit 11 discusses the metric paper sizes and weights (mass) being used by metric countries. Reference to metric will be made in this unit wherever it applies.

THE POINT SYSTEM

The point system uses two basic units:

1. The point which measures about 1/72 in.
2. The pica which is about 1/6 in. It is also equal to 12 points.

The sizes of type are given in points. The widths of lines and depth of columns may be expressed in either picas or inches. See Fig. 12-1.

Printers who work in type generation use a measuring rule called a line gauge, Fig. 12-2. It has picas and half picas on one edge. The other edge has inches and fractions of inches.

The printer must be able to convert from one measuring system to the other. Some general rules, Fig. 12-3, make the conversion simpler. Fig. 12-4 compares the millimetre with customary and printers' units.

Fig. 12-1. A typeform's size is given as so many picas high (deep) and so many picas wide. But sometimes the dimensions are given in inches.

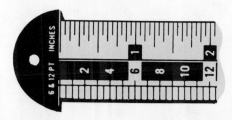

Fig. 12-2. Portion of line gauge used by printers. Note that six points are slightly larger than 1/16 in.

TO CHANGE:	TO:	MULTIPLY BY:
INCHES	PICAS	6
INCHES	POINTS	72
PICAS	POINTS	12
TO CHANGE:	**TO:**	**DIVIDE BY:**
PICAS	INCHES	6
POINTS	PICAS	12
POINTS	INCHES	72

Fig. 12-3. Rules for converting between points, picas and inches.

| PRINTERS' UNITS | | CUSTOMARY UNITS | | METRIC UNITS |
PICAS	POINTS	APPROXIMATE FRACTION (IN.)	DECIMAL (IN.)	MILLIMETRES
	1	1/64	.014	0.35
	2	1/32	.028	0.70
	3	3/64	.042	1.05
	4	7/128	.055	1.40
	5	1/16	.069	1.75
	6	5/64	.083	2.10
	7	3/32	.097	2.45
	8	7/64	.111	2.80
	9	1/8	.125	3.15
	10	9/64	.138	3.50
1	12	21/128	.166	4.20
	14	25/128	.194	4.90
	18	1/4	.249	6.30
2	24	21/64	.332	8.40
	30	53/128	.414	10.50
3	36	1/2	.498	12.60
	42	37/64	.581	14.70
4	48	85/128	.664	16.80
5	60	53/64	.828	21.00
6	72	1	.996	25.20

Fig. 12-4. Comparing different units of measure for printing. Which is the smaller unit, the point or the millimetre?

CONVERSION PROBLEMS

Using the chart in Fig. 12-3, solve the following:

1. If copy depth is 1 1/2 in., what is the depth in picas? In points?
2. Give the size, in picas, of a ticket measuring 3 1/2 by 2 in.
3. How many 60 pt. lengths can be cut from a rule 36 in. long? How much of the rule will be left over?
4. What is the area, in square inches, of a typeform 18 picas wide and 84 picas deep?
5. Add: 10 points, 8 picas, 6 points, 24 picas, 5 inches and 169 points.
6. Give the size, in inches, of a typeform set 27 picas wide by 45 picas deep.
7. Referring to Fig. 12-4, change 12 picas to millimetres.

COPYFITTING

Calculating the amount of type that can be placed in a certain space on a page is called copyfitting. The same process is used to determine how much space is needed for a manuscript containing a certain number of words or type characters. To copyfit the typographer must know:

1. How much room the type will take up.
2. How many characters are contained in the manuscript copy.

Manufacturers of type issue charts showing the number of type characters that will fit into a pica of space. This is called its "characters per pica count" or "cpp." The cpp will vary with each typeface and type size. See Fig. 12-5.

COPYFITTING PROCEDURE

Suppose that you have a space 15 picas wide by 27 picas deep to be filled with 10 pt. Bodoni type set with two points of leading (expressed 10/12) between lines. How many characters are needed to fill the space? How many words? Proceed as follows:

1. Change depth of the column from picas to points. 27 picas times 12 = 324 pts.
2. Find the depth in points that one line of type will take. 10 pt. plus 2 pt. leading = 12 pts.
3. Find the number of lines of type to fill the space. 324 divided by 12 = 27 lines.

TYPEFACE	TYPEFACE	CHARACTERS PER PICA (CPP)
10 PT.	GOUDY BOLD	2.25
10 PT.	BODONI	2.33
10 PT.	GOUDY LIGHT	3.00
8 PT.	CASLON BOLD	3.00
10 PT.	GARAMOND	2.16

Fig. 12-5. Before type can be copyfitted, one must know of characters that will fit into a pica of width.

4. Find the number of characters in one line of type. Multiply width (15 picas) by 2.33 (cpp for Bodoni) = 34.95 or 35 characters.
5. Find the number of characters needed to fill the space. Multiply 34.95 by number of lines (27) = 943.65 or 944 characters.
6. Since there are 5.5 characters in the average word, figure the number of words needed to fill the space. Divide total characters (944) by characters per word (5.5) = 171.63.

Now suppose that you have a manuscript of 1552 characters (counting letters and spaces). How much space will it fill if set in 10/14 Garamond, 20 picas wide?

1. Determine how many characters will fit in one line.
   a. Find out how many characters will fit in 1 pica (cpp). Refer to Fig. 12-5, previous page. Answer is 2.16.
   b. Multiply cpp (2.16) by line length (20 pica). Answer: 43.2 characters per line.
2. Find number of lines in the copy, Fig. 12-6.

Fig. 12-6. Type gauge simplifies finding characters per line of manuscript. Lay scale along lines and take average length. Multiply characters per line by number of lines.

Divide number of characters (1552) by the number that will fit in one line (43.2) = 35.92 or 36.
3. Find the depth of 36 lines leaded 4 pts.
   a. Multiply number of spaces between lines (35 one less than the number of lines) = 140 pts.
   b. Multiply number of lines (36) by point size (10) = 360.
   c. Add leading and type size = 500 pts.

4. Convert the points to picas. 500 pts. divided by 12 = 41.66 or 42 pts. = depth of column.

COPYFITTING PROBLEMS

Solve the following problems:

1. How many words will be needed to fill a space in a layout 12 picas by 12 picas? Use 10/12 Garamond type.
2. If the space is 18 picas by 30 picas and the type 10 pt. Goudy Light, how many characters will be needed to fill the space? How many words?
3. How many words will be needed to fill a space 20 picas wide by 24 picas deep using 10 pt. Bodoni?
4. A manuscript contains 3703 words. How many lines of copy will it yield if the type is 10 pt. Goudy Light and the line length is 15 picas?

CUTTING PAPER

Some calculations must be made when cutting stock so that waste is kept to the smallest amount possible. Division is used to figure the number of press sheets that can be cut from a larger stock size.

Consider the following problem:

Determine how many 3 x 5 in. press sheets can be cut from a stock sheet 17 in. by 22 in.

The formula is:

$$\frac{\text{Dimensions of stock sheet}}{\text{Dimensions of the press sheet}} = \text{no. of pieces cut}$$

In this formula there are two methods of dividing — the vertical method and the horizontal. In the vertical method, numbers on the bottom are divided into the numbers directly above:

$$\frac{\overset{5}{\cancel{17}} \times \overset{4}{\cancel{22}}}{3 \times 5} = 5 \text{ times } 4 = 20 \text{ pieces}$$

In the criss-cross method, the lower number is divided into the number above the line diagonally, thus:

$$\frac{\overset{3}{\cancel{17}} \times \overset{7}{\cancel{22}}}{3 \times 5} = 21 \text{ pieces}$$

The sheet will yield more pieces from the criss-cross method. Fig. 12-7 shows how the cuts would be made. The wavy line represents waste. As shown in the illustration, there is an inch of waste along one edge and two inches of waste along the other edge. Sometimes, large pieces of waste can be used for other printing jobs. Fig. 12-8 shows how the printer would make the cuts in the stock.

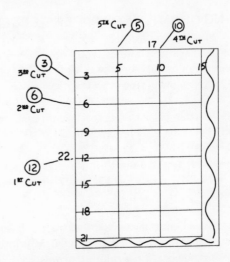

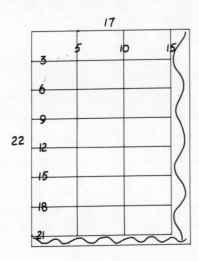

Fig. 12-7. Printers layout or "cutting chart" shows how 21 pieces of 3 x 5 in. stock are cut from a 17 x 22 in. sheet.

Fig. 12-8. Printer will mark up the "cutting chart" to show the order in which cuts are to be made.

CUTTING METRIC SIZES

Metric paper sizes have been standardized to minimize waste. Fig. 12-9 shows a metric sheet measuring 594 mm by 420 mm. It is close to the customary size, 17 x 22 in. It will produce 48 pieces of a press sheet measuring 74 by 105 mm. It has been divided by the criss-cross method.

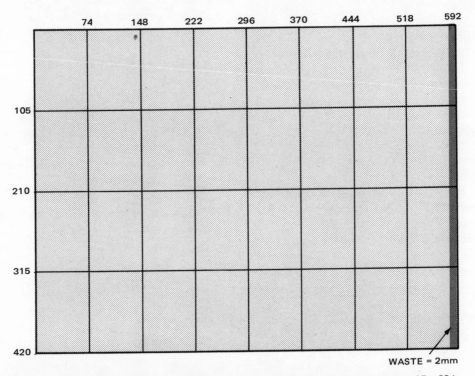

Fig. 12-9. Cutting chart for a metric size sheet. It is an ISO size A2, nearly the same as 17 x 22 in. Here it is divided into 32 size A7 sheets. A full sheet size is 594 mm by 420 mm.

FINDING QUANTITY OF PAPER NEEDED

From earlier computations, you know how many press sheets can be cut from the stock size. On a press run of 250, how many stock sheets are needed?

1. Since you can cut 21 press sheets from each stock sheet, divide the total press run by 21.
250 divided by 21 = 11 19/21.
2. Convert the part of a sheet to the next whole number. Thus, 12 sheets of 17 by 22 in. stock are needed.

Printers will also allow some extra stock since some copies of the job will be spoiled in printing, folding or binding. On the printing of this book, for example, an allowance of 6 percent was made for such spoilage.

FINDING PAPER COSTS

Most paper is sold by the pound. Catalog listings usually quote paper price per hundredweight (cwt). To work out paper prices you must be familiar with the way weights of papers are listed. For example: Bond 17 x 22 — 20 means that 500 sheets of 17 x 22 Bond will weigh 20 lb. When an "M" follows the last number, it means the weight is for 1000 sheets.

Paper is sold in various quantities. A broken ream is less than 500 sheets; a ream or package is 500 sheets; a carton contains the nearest even number of reams to about 125 lb. Price will vary according to quantity. The larger the quantity purchased the less the price per pound. More information on the kinds and sizes of papers will be found in Unit 11, Paper, Ink and Other Materials.

PROBLEM

Find the cost of 25 stock sheets of 17 x 22 — 20 Bond when it is listed at $25.25 per cwt.

1. Use the following formula to find the weight of 25 sheets:

$$\frac{\text{Number of stock sheets} \times \text{twice ream weight}}{1000}$$

= weight of number of sheets

$$\frac{25 \times 40}{1000} = 1 \text{ lb. of paper}$$

2. Find the cost by multiplying the weight of the sheets by the cost per pound. Convert the price per hundredweight to cost per pound by moving decimal point two places to the left.

$25.25 per cwt. = .2525 per lb.

Envelopes are sold by the carton. The catalog listing will indicate how many thousand envelopes are in each carton.

SCALING PHOTOGRAPHS

Usually, a proportion scale is used to scale photographs, or the diagonal method is used. However, it can also be worked out mathematically with a formula:

Product of the means = product of the extremes.

For example, a photograph 8 in. wide and 10 in. high must fit in a smaller space. The 8 in. width must reduce to 5 in. What will the height be when reduced?

The old width is to the new width as the old height is to the new height (unknown):

8: 5 as 10: X(unknown)
Multiply outer numbers (extremes) = 8X
Multiply inner numbers (means)   = 50
8X = 50
X (unknown) = 6.25 in. or 6 1/4 in.

QUIZ — UNIT 12

1. A point is _____ in., and 12 picas equal about _____ inch.
2. What two pieces of information must a typographer have to fit copy?
3. "Cwt." means _____.
4. What is the weight per 1000 sheets of a paper listed as Bond 17 x 22 — 20?

GRAPHIC ARTS ACTIVITIES

1. Using the tools of seven different graphic arts processes.
2. Working with and becoming more familiar with many graphic arts materials.
3. Learning basic printing processes by doing them yourself.

Printing processes take on greater meaning when you can become personally involved in them. This unit will present "hands-on" activities closely related to tasks performed in the graphic arts industry.

LINOLEUM BLOCK PRINTING

Preparation of linoleum block plates or cuts for printing require only a type-high linoleum block (.918 in.) and some carving tools. See Fig. 13-1.

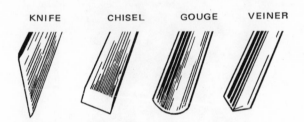

Fig. 13-1. Linoleum block carving tools are designed for special cutting tasks.

Linoleum blocks can be purchased already mounted type-high, or linoleum can be bought separately and glued to wood blocks.

DESIGNS

Keep designs for linoleum block printing simple. Lines should be heavy and the illustrations should have bold masses of black and white. See Fig. 13-2. Additional design suggestions are shown in Fig. 13-3.

REVERSING THE DESIGN

Once selected, the design must be carved in reverse so it will print correctly. There is a simple method of reversing the design.

Fig. 13-2. This bookplate design is suitable for linoleum block printing.

1. Place a piece of carbon paper on the back of the design with carbon side up.
2. Place the design face up and trace over it with a pencil or ball point pen. This imprints the design on the back of the sheet but in reverse.
3. Transfer the design to the linoleum block, Fig. 13-4. Use a sheet of carbon paper, carbon side down, and trace from the reverse side of the design.

If carbon paper does not produce a design that is clearly visible, use white dressmakers' carbon paper.

CARVING

If you have never carved linoleum blocks before, practice on a piece of scrap to see how the tools

Fig. 13-3. Some suggestions for linoleum block design.

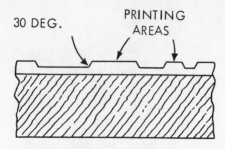

Fig. 13-5. When outlining design, make cuts at an angle of about 30 deg.

Keep tools sharp. Dull chisels are harder to control and tend to push the linoleum instead of cutting it.

The completed design can be proofed on a regular proof press. Examine the proof carefully to see if additional material must be removed. Clean the linoleum block and make corrections.

Lock up the linoleum block as you would foundry type. This is described in Unit 4. Print the design in a regular press. Fig. 13-6 shows a print made from a linoleum block.

work. The first step in carving is to outline the pattern with a carving knife. Work at an angle of about 30 deg. to provide a supporting shoulder as shown in Fig. 13-5.

Using the gouge, pare away the linoleum close to the lines. The veiner is used to tool narrow grooves in

Fig. 13-4. Use carbon paper to trace designs onto block.

the printing surface. The chisel is used to clear away larger areas. Take only shallow cuts. Be careful not to dig into the printing area. In nonprinting areas, linoleum should be removed to a depth of 1/16 in.

Fig. 13-6. Print made from linoleum plate. Note that all image areas are heavy lines or shapes.

MAKING RUBBER STAMPS

A second method of producing a relief printing plate with little equipment is to make a rubber stamp or a rubber printing plate. The procedure for making the matrix is almost identical to that used for making a sterotype or an electrotype. The only difference is the materials used.

Fig. 13-7. Type is locked up near the center of the special chase. Use metal furniture as heat will dry out wood.

PREPARE MOLD

1. Set type for the word or words that will make up the stamp.
2. Lock the type in the special chase that comes with the stamp press, Fig. 13-7. Use type-high bearers around the type. These can be a 12 pt. brass rule cut to the same length as the type line or lines.
3. Heat the rubber stamp press to the temperature specified by the manufacturer.
4. Cut a section of matrix material to size so that it will cover type lines and bearers. Bearers are type-high leading around a typeform. Matrix material is a special thermosetting plastic. It will soften during the first minute or so of the molding cycle. Then, further heat and pressure harden it to produce a permanent mold or matrix.
5. Place the matrix materials over the typeform and set the chase in the rubber stamp press. Use shims, if needed, to bring the form up to the proper height.
6. Lower the clamps into the matrix-forming position as shown in Fig. 13-8. Leave in this position for length of time recommended by the manufacturer.
7. After the proper time has elapsed, remove the chase and matrix from the press. Carefully pry the

Fig. 13-8. Rubber stamp press has been set in matrix-forming position.

Fig. 13-9. Checking completed plastic matrix.

mold off the typeform. Check the mold image as shown in Fig. 13-9.

PREPARE THE RUBBER STAMP

1. Cut a piece of rubber stamp gum to the correct size. It should be about 1/8 in. larger than the typeform.
2. Dust the gum with matrix release powder. This will assure release of the stamp from the matrix after forming and vulcanizing.
3. Place the rubber stamp gum over the matrix.
4. Place matrix and rubber on a compensating block. This is a metal block which provides the same thickness in the press as the type chase.
5. Place the compensating block, matrix and rubber stamp gum in the press and clamp it as in the matrix-forming operation.
6. Allow it to remain in the press for the time recommended by the manufacturer.
7. Remove the formed and vulcanized stamp and carefully pull the stamp away from the matrix, Fig. 13-10.

Fig. 13-10. Top. Rubber stamp is being removed from matrix. Bottom. Matrix can be compared to completed stamp. The stamp is in reverse.

8. Trim away excess rubber.
9. Mount the rubber on a piece of stamp cushion molding using rubber cement.
10. Trim molding to correct size, Fig. 13-11.
11. Sand the ends of the mounting stock and stain to match color of the molding mount.

Fig. 13-12. With a ballpoint pen or pencil, trace over design to produce reversal. Carbon paper is underneath. Carbon side is placed up.

Fig. 13-11. Cushion molding is sawed to proper length by hand.

12. If the rubber stamp is to be used in a printing press, mount it on a block to make it type-high.

SAMMY SAFETY SAYS:

Fig. 13-13. Going over reversed design with a reproducing pen applies a greasy surface to design. Grease attracts ink.

"In working around a hot rubber stamp press be careful not to get burned. Always wear heavy gloves when handling hot objects."

PRODUCING A LITHOGRAPHIC PRINT

It is possible for you to produce a lithographic print, even without offset printing equipment. If offset equipment is available, it is much easier.

You will need a design, some carbon paper, pencils, litho-reproducing pencil and a direct image plate.

1. Make a reverse of the design, Fig. 13-12. Place a piece of carbon paper, carbon side up, underneath the design. Trace the design.
2. Flop the design. The carbon will have created a reverse of the design. Trace the reversed design, again using carbon paper, onto a direct image plate.
3. With a litho-reproducing pencil, go over the lines on the direct image plate, Fig. 13-13.

4. Spread lithographic ink on a glass plate using an inking brayer.
5. Moisten the surface of the plate, Fig. 13-14.
6. Roll the inked brayer over dampened plate, Fig. 13-15. Moistened sponge will pick up any ink specks on the non-image area. If brayer picks up

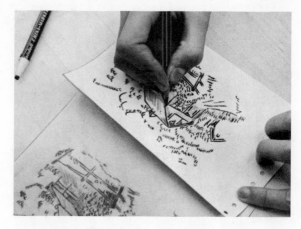

Fig. 13-14. Use a sponge to dampen direct image plate. Take care not to wet it too much. The moisture prevents non-image areas from picking up ink.

Fig. 13-15. Brayer will leave ink only on the greasy lines of the image. Wet parts repel ink.

too much water it will not transfer the ink to the plate. Excess water may be rolled out on a sheet of newspaper.

7. Place direct image plate in an etching press, Fig. 13-16 or a proof press. Lay press paper on top of

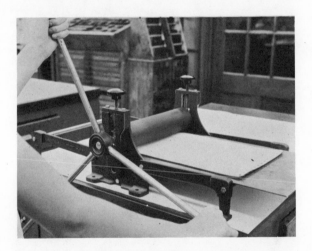

Fig. 13-16. Etching press transfers image to press sheet. Proof press can be used also but plate must be blocked up to type-high.

Fig. 13-17. Pull press sheet carefully away from plate. Place the sheet under a weight to straighten it.

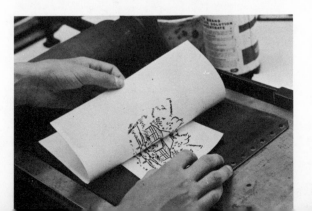

Fig. 13-18. Compare finished print with the image on the lithographic plate.

image and make an impression. Run the plate and paper through the press under slight pressure.

8. Carefully pull print and plate apart, Fig. 13-17.

9. Examine print, Fig. 13-18.

MAKING AN INTAGLIO PRINT

Intaglio printing requires large, expensive equipment usually found only in a commercial plant. Seldom is it possible to work with such equipment in a graphic arts department of a school.

But we can find out about the basic steps in such printing by making a drypoint etching. A drypoint etching is an intaglio print made by hand, using a sharp-pointed instrument to tool or scratch a design into a plate.

Plate material may be transparent celluloid or plastic such as sheet acetate. Cleared X-ray film is also satisfactory.

To make a drypoint etching:

1. Find or draw a suitable design. It should be one that lends itself to line reproduction, Fig. 13-19.

Fig. 13-19. Any art that can be reproduced with lines is suitable for drypoint etching.

2. Select an etching tool. A sharp steel needle, such as a phonograph needle, will do. It should be fitted into a wooden handle or be clamped in a pin vise. An old dental tool, sharpened to a point, also works well, Fig. 13-20.

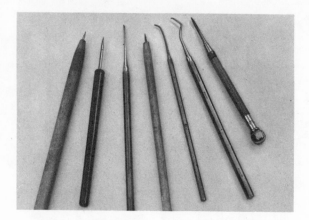

Fig. 13-20. Old dental picks make good etching tools.

3. Place the film over the design and tape it in place along one edge.
4. With the needle, scratch in the lines. Use a series of short scratches rather than long ones. For dark areas, crosshatching of lines will make the area print darker.
5. Check the engraving occasionally. Scratches will be easier to see if you slide a black or dark-colored paper between the plate and the design as shown in Fig. 13-21.

Fig. 13-21. It is easier to check progress of the etching from a darkened background.

To make prints from the completed film:

1. Prepare the paper for printing. This is an important step. Select a piece of antique book paper. Cut it to correct size for your prints. Soak the sheets in water, Fig. 13-22, and place them between pieces of blotter stock. Place a weight on the stack to keep the sheets flat. Let them sit for an hour before using.
2. While the paper is conditioning, prepare the ink.
   a. Select an etchers' ink or any other soft-bodied printing ink.
   b. Add to it a small quantity of plate oil or ink reducer to reduce the tack (stickiness). Work in the plate oil with an ink knife, Fig. 13-23.

Fig. 13-22. Wet the paper thoroughly.

Fig. 13-23. If ink is too heavy bodied, mix in plate oil with an ink knife.

3. Ink the film when the paper is ready. With a piece of lint-free cloth work the ink into the etched lines. Dab, do not slide or rub the cloth over the film. Fill all the lines with ink.
4. Remove the surplus ink from the areas between

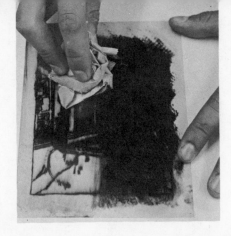

Fig. 13-24. Use straight strokes with clean cloth or toweling to remove ink.

the lines. In rotogravure, the doctor blade does this. In drypoint etching, the ink must be wiped with paper toweling or a clean lint-free cloth. Also, wipe in straight strokes to avoid removing ink from the scratches, Fig. 13-24. When most of the ink is removed, place a drop of plate oil on the palm of your hand and finish wiping the plate with your palm.

5. Make a print in the etching press, Fig. 13-25.
6. Examine the print, Fig. 13-26.

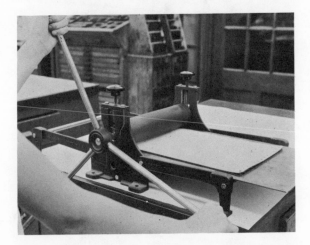

Fig. 13-25. Use considerable pressure on etching press to make print. Bed the plate (film) on a piece of felt.

Fig. 13-26. Compare print with plate.

To make additional prints, repeat all steps except the scratching of the plate. Fig. 13-27 shows additional designs.

HEAT TRANSFER PRINTING

Also called sublimation printing, the heat transfer printing process causes a printed image to move from paper onto cloth, such as a T-shirt. The process works best on 100 percent polyester fabric but will also work well on cotton and polyester blends.

MATERIALS AND EQUIPMENT

In addition to printing equipment and materials already in the graphic arts department, the following items will be needed:

1. Sublimation or heat transfer inks. Under heat, the solids vaporize and the dyes penetrate the fibers of the cloth.
2. A heating device to transfer the inks. An electric iron or a dry mount press will do the job.

Fig. 13-27. Any line art may be considered for conversion to a drypoint etching.

PROCEDURE

1. Wash the cloth or garment to remove all sizing. Dry thoroughly.
2. Print the design wrong reading using the offset method, Fig. 13-28. Commercial printers use a special transfer paper. However, a good grade of offset paper will work well enough. If you plan for more than one color, print all of the colors on the transfer sheet. Allow the inks to dry

Fig. 13-28. Design placed on sheet of offset paper is dry and ready for transfer to a T-shirt.

Fig. 13-29. Design has been transferred with application of heat.

before proceeding to step 3.

3. Set the dry mount press to about 390 deg. F (199 C). If using an iron, set the heat control for cotton. Do not use steam.
4. Place a sheet of white cardboard under the first layer of cloth. This prevents the design from transferring to the other layer or layers.
5. Place the design face down on the cloth and fasten it with tape or pins. Do not allow the design to slip.
6. Place a sheet of clean paper over the transfer sheet. Never allow the iron or dry mount plate to touch the transfer paper.
7. Apply the heat for about 15 or 20 seconds.
8. Carefully lift one corner of the transfer paper to see if the design has transferred.
9. If it has not transferred, replace sheets carefully and heat a little longer. Check again.
10. When the design has transferred, separate the transfer paper from the cloth. The process is completed and the garment or material is ready to use, Fig. 13-29.

Heat transfer inks do not appear as brilliant on the transfer paper as do regular inks. However, they will become more colorful after being transferred to the cloth.

BOOKBINDING

In this activity, you will learn how to collect folded sheets or pages and case bind them. You will sew the sheets together by hand, make endsheets, make a hardcover and case the book in the cover.

To prepare the sheets:

1. Take between 10 and 15 sheets of 5 1/2 in. by 8 1/2 in. paper and hand fold each sheet in half. Use a bone folder.
2. Gather the sheets by tucking each sheet into the fold of the preceding sheet. See Fig. 13-30.

Fig. 13-30. Assembling folded sheets. Slide each folded sheet into the center of the book.

To prepare the endsheets:

1. Use a special endsheet paper. Cut one large, double endsheet the same length as the book sheets, 5 1/2 in., but twice the width plus 1/2 in. Check the size before cutting. It should measure 5 1/2 in. by 9 in.
2. Cut two more endsheets. Make each the size of a

single sheet of your book page, 4 1/4 in. by 5 1/2 in.

3. Cut a strip of binding cloth, 2 1/2 in. by 5 1/2 in.
4. Glue the cloth to the two small endsheets as shown in Fig. 13-31. Use bookbinders' glue or a suitable white paste.

Fig. 13-33. Use awl to punch holes through folds of sheets.

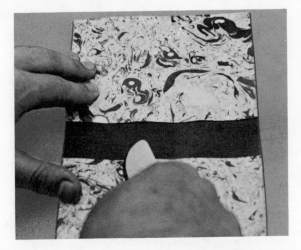

Fig. 13-31. Lay cloth flat and glue endpapers to it.

5. Fold both sets of endsheets and place them over the folded body sheets. Endsheets without the cloth strip go on first, then the clothbound set. Place the finished side of the cloth to the inside.
6. Place the sheets in a V-trough, Fig. 13-32, as shown in Fig. 13-33.
7. Make a pencil mark 1/2 in. from each end and divide up the remaining space into four equal spaces. Use a pencil to mark spots for five holes.
8. Using an awl, punch holes at each mark. See Fig. 13-33.
9. Sew the sheets together with linen or nylon

thread as shown in Fig. 13-34. Tie a good knot.
10. Apply a piece of backing flannel or super cloth at the fold. This material should be about 3/4 in. wide and 1/2 in. shorter than the length of the book, Fig. 13-35.
11. With a paper cutter, trim three sides of the book.

To make the case or hardcover:

1. Cut two pieces of binder's board (heavy chipboard type of material). Make them 1/4 in. longer than

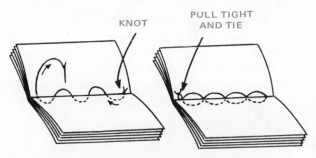

KNOT   PULL TIGHT AND TIE

Fig. 13-34. Procedure for sewing through book pages and endsheets.

the book (5 1/4 in. plus 1/4 in.) and 1/8 in. narrower (4 1/8 in.).
2. Cut a piece of binding cloth according to the dimensions shown in Fig. 13-36.
3. Mark the wrong side of the binding cloth for placement of the cover boards. Glue the two boards in place.
4. Cut off the corners of the binding cloth at a

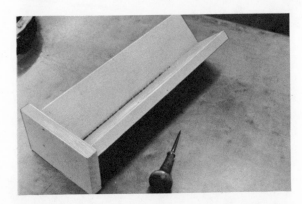

Fig. 13-32. Trough made of wood holds folded sheets during perforating.

Fig. 13-35. Super cloth (light-colored strip) is added to strengthen the back of the book.

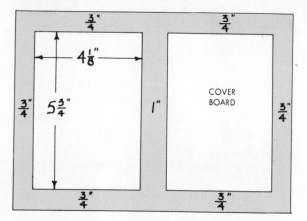

Fig. 13-36. Layout shows dimensions of cover cloth and proper positions of the cover boards.

diagnoal as shown in Fig. 13-37. Leave about 1/4 in. of material from the corner.

5. Apply glue to one of the overhanging edges of the binding cloth.

6. Wrap the edge over the cover boards. Use a bone

Fig. 13-37. Clip corners of cover cloth.

folder to get a neat fold. Glued edges will adhere to the cover board. Tuck in the corner as shown in Fig. 13-38.

7. Repeat step 6 for each edge.

8. If the shop has a gold-stamping machine, set type for the book title. When the glue has dried, stamp the title on the cover, Fig. 13-39.

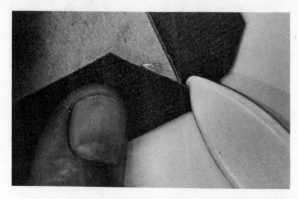

Fig. 13-38. Corner of cover cloth is tucked in along the edges of the cover board to form a "nicked" corner.

Fig. 13-39. Title is stamped on cover before being attached to the book.

Casing the book is the final operation in binding. This is the bookbinder's term for gluing the cover onto the sewed book. To case a book:

1. Starting at the front of the book, place a sheet of waxed paper or newspaper between the endsheets.

2. Apply a light coat of glue to the outer endsheet as shown in Fig. 13-40.

3. Position the cover over the endsheet, Fig. 13-41, and press endsheet and cover together. (Be sure to crease the cloth binding at the hinge.)

Fig. 13-40. Outside face of endsheet is glued to receive cover.

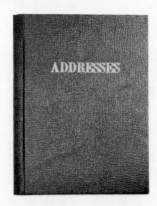

Fig. 13-43. Bookbinding is completed.

MAKING PAPER

Even though making paper in a modern mill is a highly technical process, you can get a good idea of how wood pulp is formed in sheets with some simple equipment.

The basic material is wood pulp which can be obtained from a paper mill. Dried pulp is kept on hand for experimental purposes by many graphic arts departments. Some schools substitute tissue paper which can be shredded and mixed with starch.

To make paper:

1. Place some dried wood pulp in a pan or tub. Capacity of the container should be about two gallons (7.6 litres). Fill the pan about half full of water.
2. With an eggbeater or a drill fitted with a mixing rod, stir the solution until it is free from lumps. See Fig. 13-44.
3. Using a mold and deckle, Fig. 13-45, form a quantity of the wet pulp into a sheet.
   a. Slide the combined mold and deckle into the pulp solution at a slight angle until completely submerged.
   b. Bring mold and deckle to a flat position slowly, shaking it from side to side to distribute the pulp evenly.

Fig. 13-44. Mix pulp with a beater until smooth.

Fig. 13-41. Cover is positioned over glued endsheet.

4. Turn the book over and repeat steps 1, 2 and 3 on the back of the book.
5. Place the book between two heavy metal plates with turned edges, Fig. 13-42. Place assembly in a press to dry. Drying will take several hours. Completed book is shown in Fig. 13-43.

Fig. 13-42. Book is placed between metal plates with turned edges. This puts a crease in the binding at the hinges.

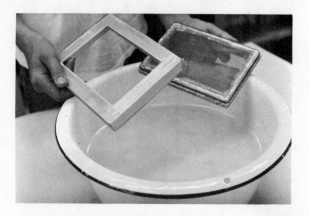

Fig. 13-45. Mold and deckle are combined and dipped into solution to pick up a thick layer of pulp fiber.

c. Place the mold on a table and lift the deckle from the mold.

d. Place the mat of newly formed paper on a blotter. This is called couching, Fig. 13-46.

4. Place several blotters on either side of the new sheet and put it in a press, Fig. 13-47. Tighten the

Fig. 13-46. Deckle is turned over to dump the newly formed sheet onto a blotter.

Fig. 13-47. Use a press to remove water from new sheet.

press to squeeze out most of the moisture.

5. Remove blotters and sheet from the press. Place the sheet between two sheets of smooth, uncoated paper.

6. Iron the paper dry with a warm iron, Fig. 13-48.

7. For about a second, submerge the paper in a 5 percent glue and water mixture. This sizes the sheet so you can write on it in ink. See Fig. 13-49.

8. Again, iron the sheet dry with a warm iron. Fig. 13-50 shows a completed sheet of handmade paper.

Fig. 13-48. Dry the sheet with a warm iron.

Fig. 13-49. Solution of water and glue provides a "sealer" so fibers are not too absorbent.

Fig. 13-50. Dried paper is now fairly stiff and usable.

TERMS TO KNOW

AD COPY: The typed message prepared for an advertisement.

ADVERTISING: Art and craft of calling attention to products, services and needs of people for purpose of influencing them to buy the products and services.

AGAINST THE GRAIN: Going the opposite way in which fibers of a sheet of paper lay.

ALBUMEN PLATE: In lithography, a printing plate coated with bichromated egg sensitizing solution.

ALIVE: A typeform from the time it is set until it is ready to be distributed.

AMPERSAND: Name for the character "&."

ANTIQUE FINISH: Paper with a rough, soft, uneven surface; uncalendered.

APPRENTICE: One who is taking the required course of formal instruction to become a journeyman under trade organization rules.

ARABIC NUMERAL: Any of the number symbols, 0, 1, 2, 3, 4, 5, 6, 7, 8, 9.

ASCENDER: Part of a lowercase letter which extends above the body.

ASPHALTUM: Tar-like material that protects a printing plate against acid and corrosion.

AUTOMATIC FEEDER: Mechanical device that feeds sheets of paper into a printing press.

AUTOMATION: A system or process which operates automatically, with little human help.

BACK EDGE: Rear edge of press sheet as it goes through press.

BACKING UP: Printing the reverse side of a sheet.

BAIL: Hinged metal bands on a platen press which holds the sheets of a tympan in place.

BALANCE: In design, having elements on a layout distributed equally left and right so that the effect is pleasing.

BASIC (OR BASIS) WEIGHT: A weight classification given to a single sheet of printing paper. But the number refers to the weight of 500 sheets of a certain size.

BEARER: Type-high strips of metal placed around the typeform prepared for electrotyping.

BED: Flat metal table on a printing press which holds the type.

BELLOWS: Accordion-pleated, light-tight hood extending from the camera back to the lens board.

BENDAY: Process for adding a shaded effect through printing tiny dots as a line engraving.

BIBLE PAPER: Thin, opaque book paper which has strength and durability. Suited for printing of thick books such as Bibles.

BINDER'S BOARD: Tough, hard, smooth fiberboard used as covers for books.

BINDING: The protective covering and fastenings on a book.

BLANK: A quad, slug, piece of furniture or other material used in a typeform to make a blank space on the printed page or sheet.

BLANKET: In offset lithography, a rubber-surfaced sheet attached to the transfer cylinder of the press. It transfers the image from the printing plate to the press sheet.

BLEED: Illustration which runs off one or more edges of the page.

BLOCKING OUT: Causing certain areas of illustrations not to print.

BOND: A tough, hard-surfaced printing paper.

BOND INK: Ink used for letterpress printing on heavily sized paper.

BONE FOLDER: A piece of flat, smooth bone, 5 to 8 in. long, with rounded ends; used to hand fold sheets.

BOOK CLOTH: Tough fabric of woven fibers, paper or plastic which forms the outer covering of books.

BRAYER: Small hand roller used for spreading ink.

BURIN: Engravers' tool with an oblique point of tempered steel, used in line engraving.

BY-LINE: Line over or under an article in a newspaper which tells who wrote it.

CALENDER: Glossy surface achieved by passing paper between highly polished rollers during manufacture.

CALIFORNIA JOB CASE: Shallow drawer of many compartments used for storage of handset type.

CAMERA-READY COPY: Type and illustrations pasted up and ready to be photographed.

CAP: Printers' term for capital or capitalize.

CAPITAL LETTER: Large letter used to begin a sentence or a proper name.

CARDBOARD: Stiff, compact board made of paper and used in printing where thick, supportive materials are needed.

CASE: Shallow partitioned tray or drawer for holding type.

CASE BOUND: Book bound in stiff board cover.

CASEIN: Substance made from milk and looking like the whites of eggs; used in papermaking as a size and a paste for coated papers.

CATHODE: Negative pole apparatus used for plating electrotypes and steel dies.

CHASE: In letterpress printing, a metal frame used for lockup of typeforms.

CHINA CLAY: Very fine white clay used for loading and coating paper during manufacture.

CHIPPER: Machine which reduces pulpwood logs to chips.

CLIP ART: Preprinted illustrations designed to be cut out and pasted onto layout sheet in preparation of camera-ready copy.

COATED PAPER: Paper to which a filler has been added to give it a smooth and glossy finish.

COBALT DRIER: Ingredient of ink to speed up drying time.

COLD COLORS: Colors on the blue side of the color wheel.

COLD-SET INK: An ink which is changed to the solid state by cold rather than heat.

COLLATE: In bookbinding, to gather the signatures of a book in proper order.

COLOR PROOFS: Proof of illustrations or type being printed in more than one color.

COMBINATION PLATE: Printing plate consisting of both a line engraving and a halftone.

COMMUNICATION: The act of sending and receiving messages.

COMPOSITION: The process of setting and arranging type for printing.

COMPOSITION ROLLER: A cylinder with a metal core coated with a flexible material made up of glue, molasses, glycerine and other materials; used for inking typeforms on printing presses.

CONTINUOUS TONE COPY: A photograph; an image which

carries tone ranging from white to the darkest shadow.

CONTRAST: Difference from the whitest white to the blackest black on a photograph.

COPPER ENGRAVING: Process of etching a design on copper plates.

COPY: Manuscript or text furnished to a printer.

CORNER MARKS: Lines or marks showing the edges of a layout or printing job.

COVER: In printing, the outer protective leaves of bound or stitched booklets, magazines or similar works.

CUT: Type-high plate used for printing an illustration.

DANDY ROLLER: In papermaking, a roll with a raised design used to form a watermark on paper.

DEAD FORM: Typeform that has been printed and is waiting for type distribution.

DESCENDER: Part of lowercase letter that drops below normal line formed by the body of the type.

DIE CUT: To cut paper or other paper products to desired shape using a steel die on a printing press.

DIRTY PROOF: Proof containing many errors.

DISTRIBUTION: Act of separating type and returning characters and materials to their proper place.

DOCTOR BLADE: Round-edged steel knife used in rotogravure printing to wipe off surplus ink from the surface of the press cylinder.

DOT: In halftones, the individual element of a screened, printed image.

DRAWSHEET: Top sheet of the tympan on a printing press to which gauge pins or guides are attached.

DRIER: Substance added to printing ink to insure quick and proper drying.

DUMMY: Pages of a booklet or book made up to serve as a guide for size, shape and form of the printed piece.

EDGE GILDING: Gold leaf applied to the edge of a book.

EDGE MARBLEIZING: Painted edges on books which resemble marble.

EGGSHELL: Paper having a surface similar to that of an eggshell.

ELECTROTYPE: A copy of a typeform or another hot type printing plate made by taking an impression on wax, depositing in this mold a thin shell of copper or other metal by an electroplating process. This facing is backed with type metal.

EM: The square of the body of type; used as a unit of measurement of type matter.

EMBOSS: To produce a raised design or lettering upon a flat surface (such as paper in printing or engraving or leather in bookbinding).

EN: Unit of measurement for type matter half the width of an em but equal in depth.

ENAMEL FINISH: Surface produced on paper by coating with a mixture of China clay, satin white and casein either glossy or dull.

END SHEET: An extra sheet of paper, plain or printed, sometimes with a decorative design. It is placed between the cover and the body of a book.

ENGRAVING: The art or process of producing a design by cutting or etching the surface of wood blocks or metal plates; a halftone or line plate.

ESTIMATE: Approximate cost of a certain job of printing.

ETCHING SOLUTION: Chemical used to eat away metal in the platemaking process.

EVAPORATION: Passing of a fluid into a vapor.

EXPOSURE: Period of time during which a light-sensitive surface is exposed to light in a camera or printing frame.

FACE: The part of a type character which produces an image during printing.

FAMILY: The complete collection of all the sizes and styles of a type of the same design or name.

FEEDER: One who feeds paper into a printing press or ruling machine; a mechanical device performing the same function.

FELT SIDE: The smooth side of a sheet of paper.

FINISHER: One who attaches covers and adds ornamentation to a book after it has been sewed.

FLAT: In lithography, the assembly of photographic negatives in position on goldenrod paper, glass or vinyl. Also: in photography, monotonous in hue, shade and color; free from gloss.

FLAT BED PRESS: Any press that prints from a flat typeform.

FOCUS: Point at which light passing through lenses (of a camera) converge on photographic film or ground glass to form a sharp image.

FOLDING: To lap or lay one part of a sheet of paper over another part of the sheet.

FOLIO: Page number.

FONT: Complete assortment of type of one size and style; includes all letters of the alphabet, both large and small, points, accents and numerals.

FOOT MARGIN: The blank space at the foot or bottom of a page; also called tail margin.

FOTOSETTER: Machine designed to set type photographically on light-sensitive film.

FOUNDRY: Section of a printing plant or stereotyping house where matrices are made from typeforms and where plates and stereotypes are cast.

FOUNDRY CHASE: A chase made especially to hold forms for electrotyping and stereotyping.

FOUNTAIN: Reservoir or receptacle for ink or water on a printing press.

FOUR COLOR PROCESS: Printing done by using three primary colors, red, yellow and blue with the addition of black.

FURNITURE: Blocks of wood used for locking up typeforms and filling blank spaces in forms.

GALLEY: Flat metal tray designed to hold type after it is set.

GANGING: Various printing jobs printed together on the same sheet to be separated later by cutting them apart.

GATF (GRAPHIC ARTS TECHNICAL FOUNDATION): Association formed to do research and prepare educational materials for the graphic arts industry.

GATHER: To arrange sheets or signatures in proper order.

GAUGE PIN: A pin or piece of stamped sheet metal used on the tympan of a platen press as a paper guide.

GOLDENROD FLAT: Lithographic negatives stripped to goldenrod sheets in preparation for burning (exposing) of the lithographic plate.

GRADATION: In photographic prints, the range of tones from deepest shadow or black to whitest white or highlights.

GRAINED PLATE: In lithography, a plate having a roughened surface so it will be able to retain water while printing.

GRAPHITE: Fine dust made from carbon; used as a release in electrotyping.

GRIPPER EDGE: Leading edge of sheet which is fed into press gripper.

GRIPPERS: Metal fingers that grasp press sheet and draw it into the press.

GUMMING UP: Applying solution of gum arabic to lithographic plate to prevent oxidation of nonprinting area and to protect it during washout operations.

GUTENBERG: Man credited with invention of movable metal type.

HAIRLINE: Usually thin lines on the face of a type.

HALFTONE: A photograph that has been broken up into a fine dot pattern for printing purposes.

HEAD: Top line of a page or an inscription at the top of a page or section of a book or manuscript.

HEADBAND: A thin metal slip at top of the tympan on a platen press; also, decorative strip placed at both ends of the bound edge of a sewn book.

HIGHLIGHT: The white or near-white areas of a photograph or halftone.

HOT TYPE: Type cast from molten metal.

IMPOSING STONE: The metal or stone table on which compositors make up pages from hot or foundry type and lock it up for printing.

IMPRESSION: The pressing of the paper against the inked image during printing.

IMPRESSION CYLINDER: On a printing press, the cylinder which presses the sheet of paper against the inked image.

IMPRINT: Name or trademark of the printer or publisher, sometimes with the date and place of issue, printed on a book or other printed matter.

INTAGLIO PRINTING: Printing done from plates with the design or image etched below the surface.

INTERTYPE: Tradename of a slug-casting machine that works somewhat like the linotype.

ITALIC: Style of type with graceful curves and slanting to the right.

JOB PRINTING: Type of work, such as letterheads and envelopes, done in small commercial plants.

JOG: Straighten a stack of paper by a shuffling or vibrating process.

KERN: A part of the face of a type character which projects beyond the body or shank.

KEY: Register marks used as guides when aligning further work such as a second color.

KRAFT: A tough, strong, natural-colored paper.

LACQUER FILM: Lacquer-coated film used in making silk-screen stencils.

LAMPBLACK: One of the main ingredients of black printing inks which accounts for the color.

LAYOUT: Plan of any piece to be printed showing size and position of all the elements.

LEAD: Strip of metal two points thick used as spacing between lines of type.

LEAD CUTTER: Small machine used to cut leads, slugs and rules.

LEADER: Row of dots or dashes.

LEDGER PAPER: A strong, smooth writing paper used for record keeping.

LENS: Glass element or elements designed to focus rays of light.

LETTERPRESS PRINTING: Printing from raised type or other raised surface.

LIGATURE: Type character on which two or more letters are cast on a single body.

LINE COPY: Copy suitable for reproduction without a halftone screen. Image prints as a solid color.

LINE ENGRAVING: Etched printing plate containing only solid lines and clear areas.

LINOTYPE: Machine which uses matrices or molds to cast up whole lines of type from molten metal.

LITHOGRAPHY: Type of printing based on principle that water and oil do not mix.

LIVE MATTER: Type matter to be used; not yet printed.

LOCKUP: Process of securing type matter in chase so it can be printed.

LUDLOW: Machine for casting lines of type from handset matrices.

MACHINE COMPOSITION: Type produced on typesetting machines.

MAKE-READY: Preparation of press to get a good printing impression.

MAKEUP: The operation of making up; arrangement of type matter.

MATRIX: Brass mold used in casting letters on a typesetting machine such as a linotype.

MITER: To cut rules or borders at a 45 deg. angle for 90 deg. corners.

MONOTYPE: Typesetting machine which sets lines of individual letters.

NEGATIVES: In photography, a photographic image on film in which highlights and shadows are reversed.

NEWS INK: Ink used on an absorbent stock.

NICK: Groove in the shank of a type character in handset type. It enables the compositor to distinguish between fonts of type and tell which is the bottom of the letter.

OCR (OPTICAL CHARACTER RECOGNITION): An electronic scanner which "reads" type copy and converts it to a punched tape used for typesetting.

OFFSET: A form of lithographic printing.

OLD STYLE: Style of letter in which mechanically perfect lines are not attempted; slight contrast between light and heavy elements.

OPAQUE: In lithography, a water-base solution used to cover holes in film or block out undesirable parts of the negative.

OSHA (OCCUPATIONAL SAFETY AND HEALTH ACT): Federal law designed to legislate safety and safety awareness in all kinds of workplaces.

OVERLAY: Paper or other material added to tympan sheet to equalize impression.

OXIDATION: Drying of inks by air contact.

OZALID PRINT: Contact print made on a light-sensitive paper. It makes a positive from a positive or a negative from a negative.

PASTEUP: Attaching copy to a layout sheet so it can be photographed for printing plate.

PATENT BASE: A metal base to which electrotypes can be attached to make them type-high.

PERFORATING: Part of a printing or folding operation which makes a continuous series of short cuts or holes so the paper will tear easily.

PHOTOCOMPOSITION: Method of setting type photographically on light-sensitive paper.

PHOTOENGRAVING: Printing plate made by photographically reproducing an image on a light-sensitive plate and then etching it so that a dot pattern is produced in relief.

PHOTOLITHOGRAPHY: Process of producing pictures and type for lithography by camera.

pH VALUE: The degree of acidity or alkalinity measured on a scale calibrated from 0 to 14 with 7 being the neutral point.

PICA: Unit of measure for printing which is equal to 1/6 in.

PIGMENT: The coloring matter in ink.

PLANOGRAPHY: Any of the processes of printing from a flat surface.

PLATEN PRESS: Printing press in which the impression is made when a flat surface called the platen presses the paper against the type.

POINT SYSTEM: Printer's system of measurement based on the point which is equal to 1/72 in.

POSITIVE: Photographic image in which highlights and shadows are the same as the original.

PROCESS COLOR INK: Special transparent inks used in four color printing and consisting of three primary colors (magenta, yellow and cyan).

PROOF: A trial printing impression used for examination and correction of errors.

Terms to Know

PUBLISH: The act of printing for the purpose of offering the printed piece for sale.

PULP: Particles of processed wood or other vegetable fiber used to make paper.

QUAD: Piece of metal, less than type-high, used as a spacer in setting type.

RAG CONTENT PAPER: Paper made from material in which there is some cloth fibers.

REAM: Unit of quantity in paper, usually 500 sheets.

REDUCER: A liquid or paste used in printing inks to lessen their stickiness.

REGISTER: Exact positioning of a second color printed with another color.

RELIEF PRINTING: Printing from characters or designs that are raised above the surrounding surface.

REVERSE LETTERING: White lettering on a printed or dark background.

ROTARY PRESS: A printing press using curved printing plates.

ROTOGRAVURE: Mass produced gravure printing using a rotary press.

ROUTER: A machine used for the purpose of reducing the height of parts of a printing plate.

RUN: Number of sheets to be printed.

SANS SERIF: Type style having no serifs.

SCALING: Method of determining the enlargement or reduction size of illustrations.

SCORE: Deforming heavy sheets with a bar so that they are easier to fold.

SCREEN: Film used to break up continuous tones into graduated dot patterns.

SERIF: Fine lines or cross-strokes found at the top and bottom of Roman typefaces.

SETOFF: Transfer of ink from freshly printed sheet to the back of another sheet.

SHADOW: Dark areas of a photograph or printed picture.

SIGNATURE: A section of folded pages from a book.

SIZED PAPER: Paper coated to seal its fibers against soaking up too much ink.

SLUG: A lead over 6 pt. thick.

SLUG CASTING MACHINE: Typesetting machine which sets a complete line of type in one piece or slug.

SMASH: In bookbinding, to compress the folded signatures of a book to take the swell out of the back of the book.

SOLID MATTER: Type matter without leads or slugs between the lines.

SQUEEGEE: Scraper with a rubber blade used to force ink or paint through a silk screen.

STAMP: To impress or imprint with some mark or design using pressure; the instrument used to make an impression.

STAPLE: To fasten sheets together with wire staples.

STEREOTYPE: A duplicate printing plate or typeform cast from a paper matrix.

STOCK: Paper.

STONE: Worktable with stone or steel top used in letterpress printing.

STRAIGHT MATTER: Type composition set in plain, ordinary paragraph form.

SULPHITE PULP: Wood pulp produced by the sulphate process.

THERMOGRAPHY: Method of raising printed impression by heating special powder sprinkled over inked impression while it is wet.

TINT: Reduction of a solid color by mixing with white.

TIP-IN: A sheet printed separately and glued to another sheet in a booklet or book.

TRANSPARENCY: A transparent positive photograph.

TRIM: To cut the edges of a printed piece; also, that part of the paper which is cut away.

TYMPAN: Sheets of paper or other material placed between the impression surface of a printing press, and the paper which is to be printed.

TYPE METAL: Combination of metals, such as lead, tin and antimony, used in the casting of type.

TYPE-HIGH: Being of the exact height of type, or 0.918 in.

TYPOGRAPHY: The art of printing with type.

UNDERLAY: A piece of paper, cardboard, or the like, placed under type matter or plates, on the press. It brings type to the proper height for printing and equalizes the impression.

UNION LABEL: Trademark or label attached or printed on goods which have been produced by union labor.

UPPERCASE: Name applied to capital letters of the alphabet.

VANDYKE PRINT: A silver print, or photographic image made on inexpensive paper.

VEHICLE: The carrier used in ink for transferring the pigment to the paper.

VIBRATING ROLLER: An inking roller on a printing press which distributes ink on other rollers, or on a table, by moving back and forth endways in addition to its regular rotary movement.

VIGNETTE: A halftone or other engraving whose tones gradually fade away into the unprinted portion of the paper.

VISCOSITY: Ability of a liquid to flow.

WARM COLORS: Colors on the red side of the spectrum.

WATERMARK: A mark or design produced in some kinds of papers by pressure of the dandy roll in the wet paper as it moves through the papermaking machine.

WITH THE GRAIN: Parallel to or with the direction in which the fibers run in a sheet of paper or cardboard.

WOOD ENGRAVING: Process of cutting designs upon a block of wood, leaving the design in relief for printing.

WOOD PULP: Pulp made from wood and used in the making of paper.

WORK AND TURN: Imposing all pages of a section or signature and then printing the same form on the other side.

WORK-UP: A spot or mark on printed matter, caused by spacing material in a form working up during the press run and printing with the other matter.

WRONG FONT: Type of wrong typeface.

XEROGRAPHY: A dry printing process by the electrostatic method.

XYLOGRAPHY: The art of process of engraving on wood, or of taking impressions from wood engravings.

ZINC ETCHING: Line engraving produced on zinc.

INDEX